CONTENTS

4. Children

(i) How many? Where were they?

(ii) Children's needs/Vulnerabilities

(iii) Care of children whilst mother in prison

(iv) Did prison ask about children

(v) Worries about children

5. Visits and contact

(i) Did the children visit?

(ii) Reasons for lack of visits

(iii) How were the visits for mother and child

6. The prison experience

(i) How did these mothers experience prison? Negative and positive aspects

(ii) What do the mothers say they 'learned 'in prison if anything

(iii) Do they believe that being imprisoned will affect their desistance

(iv) In their view was their imprisonment fair

7. The effects of separation by maternal imprisonment on the children – as described by their mothers

8. Help and support, agency involvement, the role of PACT

(i) Grandmothers and family

(ii) Prison staff and the role of Prison Advice and Care Trust (PACT)

9.Post Custody

(i) Housing and eviction

(ii) Supervision post custody

(iii) Resettlement in the community

10. What helped and what could have helped in our participants' view

Short but not sweet by Lucy Baldwin and Rona Epstein

Foreword

This research report bears powerful witness to the harsh impact on women and their children of the short custodial sentences too often meted out in the name of justice. It draws attention to the ripple effects of imprisoning mothers, and the turbulence it causes in the lives of their families. This is a small-scale study but by no means unrepresentative of women's experience of the criminal justice system. Two thirds of women sentenced to imprisonment in England and Wales receive terms of six months or less, and many of them have been victims of much more serious offences than those they are accused of committing. In this study, the 17 women had served between 2- 23 weeks, none for offences involving violence, some for first offences, and between them they left a total of 50 children behind.

The voices of the women interviewed come through loud, clear and eloquent about what got them into trouble, the distress that this short period of imprisonment caused them and their children and what would help them get their lives back on track. Some women appreciated the support they received in prison that had not been available in the community – for example support to leave abusive and coercive relationships or to tackle drug or alcohol addiction. But most are bitter about what they felt was disproportionate punishment that had lasting consequences for their children, and felt that a lack of support in the community (for example mental health care or financial support) had contributed to their offending.

It is important to understand this research as exemplifying system wide failure, but its power lies in the testimony of the women who agreed to be interviewed. Many cannot understand why they did not receive a community sentence which would have enabled them to tackle the causes of their offending whilst maintaining responsibility and care for their children. From the information provided, it is hard to understand why some of these prosecutions were brought in the first place.

A decade on from Baroness Corston's report on women in the justice system, at a time when the number of women being sent to prison is again on the rise, this research adds weight and urgency to the case for reform. The Prison Reform Trust, along with many others, has been calling for concerted action at both national and local level to reduce the imprisonment of women, particularly mothers, and instead provide access to early intervention, out of court disposals and community sentencing options. This requires investment in local women's centres and services, which have suffered badly from public spending cuts and new commissioning frameworks.

I commend the authors of this timely, sensitive and well-targeted research and I welcome their endorsement of the recommendations made in the Prison Reform Trust's *Sentencing of Mothers* discussion paper. Their report will be a spur to action and I look forward to helping ensure that the voices of the women who have shared their experiences, and those of their children, will be heard and heeded in the corridors of power. Women's justice reform is long overdue and will be sweet when it comes.

Jenny Earle
Programme Director, Transforming Lives, reducing women's imprisonment,
Prison Reform Trust, June 2017

Introduction

This small-scale study, kindly part-funded by the Oakdale Trust, and supported by De Montfort University and Coventry University, comes in the 10th Anniversary year, of the ground-breaking Corston Report (2007).

The *'Corston report; a review of women with particular vulnerabilities in the criminal justice system'*[1], sought to generate an ethos and vision that would help create a 'distinct, radically different, visibly led, strategic, proportionate, holistic, women centred, integrated approach' (2007:79). The 43 recommendations of the Corston report, echoed the need for positive change in relation to women and criminal justice; that researchers, academics and practitioners had consistently called for, for more than 30 years (Carlen 1985, Gelsthorpe and Morris 2002, Hedderman and Gelsthorpe 1997, McIvor 2004, Worrall 1990). This seminal report generated great optimism, achieving cross party support, and is widely seen as a 'roadmap for women specific criminal justice reform'[2]. The key message of the report was that far fewer women ought to be sentenced to custody, and that prison ought to be reserved only for the very few women who pose a danger to the public, with community based 'alternatives to custody' sought wherever possible. However, despite widespread support for the Corston recommendations, and some real progress in some key areas, the female prison population remains 'stubbornly high'. In 2013, the then Minister of State for Justice, with responsibility for women offenders, stated:

> *'The problem of women in our penal system is a disgrace that does not belong to any one government; it is a disgrace for our society'* (House of Commons Hansard debates; 9162013)

Despite the 'commitment' of the then Minister of State, Simon Hughes MP (2014), repeated by the then Prime Minister David Cameron in February 2016, and again by the previous Secretary of State, Liz Truss in 2017; to reduce the women's prison population and make better use of community initiatives, the

---

[1] Corston, J, (2007) The Corston Report: A Review of Women with Particular Vulnerabilities in the Criminal Justice System' http://www.justice.gov.uk/publications/docs/corston-report-march-2007.pdf

[2] Corston +10. The Corston Report 10 years On. Produced by Women in Prison, supported by Barrow Cadbury Trust. http://www.womeninprison.org.uk/perch/resources/corston-report-10-years-on.pdf

women's prison population has only ever briefly reduced. The figure hovers persistently around 4000, which is double the women's prison population in England and Wales from 1995. On 17th June 2016, there were 3861 women in custody in England and Wales, as of the 9th June 2017 the number had risen to 3987.

Short prison sentences have attracted widespread criticism; many question what purpose they serve, particularly as short sentenced prisoners have the highest reconviction rates amongst adult prisoners (Ministry of Justice, 2013). Yet they continue to be imposed for low-level offences such as shoplifting, or for breach of a court order (often for an original offence, that would not have attracted a custodial sentence in the first instance). Despite widespread misgivings about short sentences, their use has continued to rise; in 1993 only a third of women entering custody were sentenced to 6 months or less. More recent figures reveal, most women in prison are serving short, or very short, sentences, or periods of remand. Seventy-two per cent are serving sentences of six months or less, over 67%, are serving 12 months or less, 56% three months or less (Ministry of Justice figures 2016). The Criminal Justice Act 2003, states that imposing a custodial sentence must only occur when an offence is 'so serious' that no other alternative can be justified. Despite this, most women in prison, (over 80%), are convicted of nonviolent offences, most often shoplifting, fraud or breach. For many, (over 25%), it will be their first offence. Many women are in prison on remand, not yet found guilty of anything, most of these women (over 70%), then go on to be given a non-custodial sentence, bringing into question the logic or necessity of their remand[3].

The Association of Prison Governors has frequently questioned the use of short sentences and asked for courts to substitute community orders for short custodial sentences. The All Party Parliamentary Group (APPG), on Women in the Penal System presented its 'Report on the Inquiry into Preventing Unnecessary Criminalisation of Women' (2015). It highlighted the severe damage' inflicted by short prison sentences on women, suggesting that '*the criminal justice system fails catastrophically when a woman ends up in prison*'. A Chief Constable informed the APPG that '*after women go to prison, their offending often goes up a notch*', recognising that women '*become trapped in cycles of multiple disadvantage*'. He stressed that short sentences were wasteful and plunged

---

[3] The   Prison: The   Facts.   Bromley   Briefings.   Summer   2016.   Prison   Reform   Trust.
http://www.prisonreformtrust.org.uk/Portals/0/Documents/Bromley%20Briefings/summer%202016%20briefing.pdf

women into further chaos, as even a brief spell in custody often leads to loss of accommodation, employment and custody of children.

The findings of this research highlight the, in the main, devastating effects these short sentences can have on mothers and their children.

A. The main aims of this research: hearing the voices of mothers who have experienced prison

We wished to give mothers who had experienced prison an opportunity to recount what had happened to them and to their children. We wanted to hear the voices of women who are too often silent.

We aimed to explore the experiences of mothers who had served short custodial sentences (12 months or less), we were interested in their views from before their sentence, during their sentence and post release.

We wished to explore the pre-existing circumstances of mothers who served short periods in custody, enquire into their experiences while in prison and to seek the mothers' view of the impact of their sentence on their children. We hoped to acquire information on the post-custodial period, how did they experience supervision after custody, what had they found helpful in coping with life after imprisonment?

We sought information on how the children 'left behind' were cared for in the absence of their mother and how they coped with the separation. We wished to learn about support for these mothers and their children, both while they were in prison and after. We hoped to learn something about the effects of such short sentences, both on the women who serve them and the children from whom they are separated. We wanted to know what were the mother's own views of the short term and the long-term effects, on themselves and their children?

Finally, we hoped to add valuable information to the existing research on mothers and imprisonment, and to offer contributions and recommendations for positive change and future research.

B. Context

Significantly, currently there are no accurate, up to date figures representing the actual number of mothers in custody (Baldwin 2015, Prison Reform Trust 2015). The figure most commonly referred to, suggests 66% will be mothers of children under 18 (Caddle and Crisp 1997). However, it is acknowledged this figure is twenty years old. There are variations and contradictions in more recent figures, as identified by the Prison Reform Trust (PRT) in their 2015 paper, 'Sentencing of Mothers',[4] which reports the MOJ had 'more recently' estimated the figure conservatively, as between 24%-31%. This figure was ascertained by matching police national computer (PNC) data, against the Department of Work and Pensions data, thereby apparently identifying accurate figures of mothers in custody, by highlighting who had an active child benefit claim at that time (MOJ, 2012). There are many reasons why this figure would not be accurate, not least because it may not include foreign national mothers, mothers who have children in care, or mothers reluctant to disclose details about their children, also in cases where mothers are not the claimant. Furthermore, as with the Caddle and Crisp figures, the PNC/MOJ acquired figures do not include mothers of older children, or grandmothers who may have been a significant or primary carer; who incidentally, are also still mothers, therefore affected by many of the same issues as younger mothers (Baldwin 2015, see also [5]). The loss of their care and support, as mothers *and* grandmothers, may have devastating effects on a vulnerable family, which already may be facing multiple challenges (Baldwin 2015). To date grandmothers have often been 'invisible' in both research and literature pertaining to women and imprisonment (ibid)[6].

The Prison Reform Trust, estimate that around 18,000 children are separated from their mothers every year. However, similarly, figures relating to children may not be accurate, as currently there is no systematic or formal recording of what happens to the children of imprisoned mothers. Again, the figures most often referred to, hail from the Caddle and Crisp 1997 study. Figures accepted by the PRT (2014), suggest then, that only 5% of these children remain in their own home, 9% are cared for by their fathers, and 14% go directly into the care of a local authority. The remaining 72% are variously located with family and friends (predominantly grandmothers) (ibid).

Mothers and Sentencing

Research from the UK and across Europe on the effects of parental imprisonment has identified many negative outcomes (Player 2005, Epstein

[4] Minson S., Nadine R., Earle, J. Sentencing of Mothers: Improving the sentencing process and outcomes for women with dependent children. Prison Reform Trust. http://www.prisonreformtrust.org.uk/Portals/0/Documents/sentencing_mothers.pdf

[5] Baldwin L. (2017), 'Grandmothering in the Context of Criminal Justice: Grandmothers in Prison and Grandmothers as Carers when a Parent is Imprisoned'. (Forthcoming)

[6]See Footnote 2 also , Baldwin (2015).

2012, Minson 2014, PRT 2014, Baldwin 2015). The imprisonment of mothers has been described as having 'wreaked havoc on family stability and children's well-being'.[7] The multinational EU-funded study *'Children of prisoners: interventions and mitigations to strengthen mental health'*; on the mental health of children of prisoners across four European countries, found that most children reported being negatively impacted by the imprisonment of a parent.[8]

The Human Rights Act 1998, in conjunction with the European Convention requires the 'rights of the child' to be considered in the potential imprisonment of a parent. The imprisonment of a parent involves the 'forcible separation' of a parent and child, therefore, interferes with the article 8 'rights of the child' (depriving the child of parental care).

When courts sentence a mother with a dependent child, the Article 8 rights of the child are engaged. This was made clear in a 2001 case, *R (on the application of P and Q) v Secretary of State for the Home Department*, concerning the prison rule which provided that babies in a Mother and Baby Unit had to leave the unit at the age of 18 months. Two mothers, P and Q, challenged the inflexible application of that rule. Lord Phillips, Master of the Rolls, said:

> *It goes without saying that since 2nd October 2000[9] sentencing courts have been public authorities within the meaning of section 6 of the Human Rights Act. If the passing of a custodial sentence involves the separation of a mother from her very young child (or, indeed, from any of her children) the sentencing court is bound ... to carry out the balancing exercise ... before deciding that the seriousness of the offence justifies the separation of mother and child. If the court does not have sufficient information about the likely consequences of the compulsory separation, it must, in compliance with its obligations under section 6(1), ask for more.* [10]

Accordingly, sentencers must:

1. Acquire information about dependent children; and

---

[7] Convery, U. and Moore, L. (2011) Children of imprisoned parents and their problems, in *Children of Imprisoned Parents*, (Ed) Peter Scharff Smith and Lucy Gampell, European Network for Children of Imprisoned Parents, Denmark.

[8] Robertson, O (2015) Child rights: some long-term perspectives, in *European Journal of Parental Imprisonment: An evolving child rights agenda*, Spring 2015.

[9] The Human Rights Act 1998 entered into force on 2 October 2000.

[10] [2001] EWCA Civ 1151), at para 79.

2. Balance the Article 8 rights of the child against the seriousness of the mother's offence.

This principle was later endorsed and re-stated in several further cases of the imprisonment of parents[11].

Epstein undertook a study in 2012 to explore how far sentencers accepted these principles, and considered the rights of the child in the sentencing of their mothers. Epstein (2012) found in her study, that despite being guided, and indeed required to do so, judges and magistrates appeared to be failing in their duty to undertake the 'balancing exercise', in which they would consider the 'rights of the child' against the necessity and appropriateness of a custodial sentence. She found that found that in 75 cases there was *"no evidence of any specific consideration of the Article 8 rights of the child,"* and that reference to the welfare of any dependent children was at best inconsistent. The sentencing council regards sole or primary care of a dependant as *'something that ought to be given mitigating consideration.".* However, as Baldwin highlights; *'mitigation in relation to the offender is very different to real consideration of the welfare of dependent children, or a consideration of the devastating long and short-term implication of the incarceration of mothers'* (2014:179;10.195).

The United Nation Bangkok Rules on Women Offenders and Prisoners[12], give guidance on gender sensitive responses in relation to remand, sentencing and post-conviction. Further, they state that *'non-custodial sentences for pregnant women and women with dependent children shall be preferred where possible and appropriate'*. Further suggesting that custodial sentences are given in only the most serious of offences, and only after taking into consideration of the best interests of the child. The Bangkok rules also request *'ensuring that appropriate provision has been made for the provision of such children'*. However, Judicial discretion allows the direction regarding the 'balancing exercise', to be ignored, something both Epstein (2012) and Minson (2014)[13] found evidence of in their research. Epstein and Minson both highlight how, on Appeal, Judges did consider the children and reduce the sentence. However, the point is, and as this

---

[11] *R (on the application of Amanda Aldous) v Dartford Magistrates' Court)* [2011] EWHC 1919 (Admin)) in the High Court; *R v Bishop* [2011] WL 844007), Court of Appeal; *R v Rosie Lee Petherick* [2012] EWCA Crim 2214, 3 October 2012

[12] Bangkok Rules on Women Offenders and Prisoners (2010). Available at: https://www.penalreform.org/wp-content/uploads/2013/07/PRI-Short-Guide-Bangkok-Rules-2013-Web-Final.pdf

[13] Minson, S. (2014) Mitigating Motherhood: A study of the impact of motherhood on sentencing decisions in England and Wales. Available at http://howardleague.org/wp-content/uploads/2016/03/mitigating-motherhood.pdf

report highlights, *'disruption and damage occurs with a sentence of any length, and the ideal outcome, would not be shorter custodial sentences, but fewer'* (Baldwin 2015).

C. Overview of the findings

Tables 1-3. See Appendix; Figures 1, 2, 3.

Table 1: Pre-custodial characteristics

Table 1 summarises the preexisting characteristics of the mothers; their ethnicity and offence details, length of sentence and the number of, and ages of their children. The table also identifies the preexisting vulnerabilities of the children as identified by the mothers.

Table 2: Custodial Experience

Table 2 identifies who cared for the children in their mother's absence, whether visits occurred, and their number. The table identifies how the mothers stated they experienced visits with their children, the health care they received in prison and who supported them.

Table 3: Post-custodial characteristics

Table 3 summarises the impact on the mothers' post custodial health and wellbeing (as identified by the mothers themselves), their situation regarding housing, and from whom the mothers say they experienced support. The table summarises the mothers' stated views on the effects of their sentence on their children, along with examples of stated positives and negatives the mothers attributed to their imprisonment.

The Participants

Perhaps one of the most striking features of this research, is that despite the fact that there were *only* 17 mothers involved in the research, these 17 were mothers to a total of **fifty children.** The children were aged between 18 months -19 years. All but one of the mothers, reported being a single parent, most had more than one dependent child (82%). All had at least one of their children living with them prior to their sentence, 43 of the fifty children were in their mother's care at the point of sentence (86%).Participants were given pseudonyms to preserve confidentiality.

Tables 1, 2 and 3, (see Appendix), as stated above, summarise the characteristics of the participants, their pre-existing circumstances, length of sentence, and a brief illustration of the impact of the sentence imposed, as described by the mothers themselves.

The participants were from diverse backgrounds, their make up being self-described as, 47% white British, 17% black British, 17% white Irish, and 6% each Welsh, Mixed Race and 'not stated'.

The mothers in the study were sentenced for periods ranging from 2 weeks to 34 weeks, all for non-violent offences. The mothers' offences included breach of a previous order, nonpayment of fines, theft, fraud, public order offences, theft from an electricity meter, and minor criminal damage. Two were civil debtors (they owed council tax), and therefore had not committed any offence, and ought not in fact have been sentenced to custody at all (see Appendix 2). In only one case in this study was the most recent offence breach of a previous order, although two women had previously been imprisoned for breach, and another had her hearing for breach of a previous order pending[14]. For five mothers (29%), this was their first offence.

All the participants reported preexisting challenges, disadvantages and vulnerabilities. Mothers reported issues concerning poverty, addiction, and physical and mental health. Fourteen of the 17 mothers (82%), told us they were experiencing mental health issues prior to their sentence, predominantly depression and anxiety. Apart from Melissa, who had additional physical health needs, all the mothers who were previously prescribed anti-depressants, experienced delays in receiving medication; which several mothers felt left them feeling 'worse' or even 'suicidal'. The longest delay reported was 3 ½ weeks. Many also suffered physical ill health; one has epilepsy, one suffered troubling menopausal symptoms, three were pregnant and one was diabetic. Two mothers miscarried in prison, one after bleeding in her cell for *'hours'*, eventually miscarrying in an ambulance on the way to hospital, *'in handcuffs'*.

---

[14] Most of the participants in this study were sentenced prior to Transforming Rehabilitation (TR) and therefore had not been subject to the minimum 12-month licence supervision period that they would be under current legislation, which we suspect would present a very different picture in relation to breach and cycles of imprisonment.

Participants described to us both good and bad examples of healthcare and emotional support in prison, one described the nursing staff as *'angels'*, another credits a *'good'* probation officer with saving her life. Others told us, *'staff weren't bothered'*, this view was contradicted by another mother however, who told us she found the prison staff, *'supportive and kind'*. Post custodial staff and supervision staff were described in both positive and negative terms, one supervisor for example was heavily praised, described as *'wonderful'*, and helpful in terms of preparing a mother for work. However, another was described as *'useless and not bothered'*. What became very clear, was that there appeared little consistency in the mothers' feedback in relation to their experiences of prison and supervisory staff. However, staff from the Prison Advice and Care Trust (PACT), received glowing and consistently positive feedback from the mothers who engaged with them.

Poverty was a feature in several of the mothers' lives, with some stating it had a **direct** impact on their offending, with at least two mothers describing offending to meet their children's needs or expectations. For example, Michelle stated, '*I was struggling, really struggling to pay my bills – there needs to be more support for single mums. I knew loads of mums in prison who were just trying to find ways to manage'*. Another mother shoplifted nappies and formula. Lily and Clare were both imprisoned for council tax debt, neither had ever encountered the criminal justice system (CJS) before and found the whole experience particularly difficult.

Almost all the mothers in the study described finding some aspect of their period in custody as *'traumatic'*, *'painful'* and *'heartbreaking'*. This was fundamentally due to being separated from their children, some for the first time, and some for the whole prison term, either because they received no visits, one visit only or few visits. Many of the mothers felt that the distance and cost of travelling, what were in the main long distances, prohibitive. Declaring them *'too far'*, *too expensive'*, and *'too difficult'* in terms of their emotions. Some mothers reported their children were afraid of the prison dogs. Only one mother alluded to attempting to claim travel expenses by an assistance scheme, but reported her family abandoned it as *'too complicated'*. Where visits did occur, mothers described them as *'painful'*, *'very upsetting' and 'emotionally exhausting'*, sometimes for the children as well as themselves. For these reasons, several mothers made the decision not to allow further visits. Ethel stated she felt that the visits *'were like hospital visits'*, she felt guilty *'bringing them to a prison'*. She goes on to say that she was *'heartbroken'* when her children left, and suggested it might be easier on a short sentence *'not to see them'*. However, she stated this feeling made her feel *'torn, because you miss them and they miss you'*. Sandra, a mother of 5, and mother to the youngest child attached to the study (3 months when sentenced), did not receive any visits whilst she was in prison, *'not even the baby'*. This she felt had resulted in their mother/child bond being broken. Another mother, of a four-year-old boy, described visits as 'ok', she felt she was lucky as she was *'local'*, and told her son mummy was *'at work'*, which was accepted by the child; who fared well in the visits, although the mother stated she did not. One mother who was *'relying on social services to manage the visits'* told us she waited 5 months for a visit, and '*even then, only two came, because social services failed to make arrangements'*. Several mothers described issues with contact other than visits, particularly those whose children were separated and located with different carers. Although all managed to stay in contact with their children, many found it challenging, expensive and stressful. PACT facilitated visits for two mothers.

Care of the Children

As previously found by Corston and others, the mothers in this study too, were pre-occupied and anxious about the welfare of their children. Even the mothers who were content with their childcare arrangements felt anguish and anxiety at being away from them. For the mothers, this did not appear diluted by the shortness of the sentence. One mother stated, *'being away from my kids broke my heart, I knew they'd be ok with their dad, but you still worry as the mum, don't you?'*

All the mothers had at least one child living with them prior to their sentence, seven were already in care. Most of the children in the study were displaced to various carers, which included aunts, fathers, elder siblings, friends, and paternal and maternal grandmothers. Several sibling groups were spilt up between multiple fathers and grandparent carers, this was a particular source of great anxiety to the mothers: one group, left in the care of an aunt, were latterly placed in care. Mothers spoke about the *'lack of support'*, for those caring for their children, a further source of anxiety and guilt. Particularly for the three mothers whose 17-year-old daughters were caring for their younger siblings – two of whom left full time education to do so. Mothers of at least two older children (16, and 17), felt their older children were left without formal support or supervision. One of the mother's 16-year-old daughter became pregnant whilst her mother was in prison, something the mother *'felt sure'* would not have occurred if she had been *'home'* to supervise her. The baby was adopted. We believe the

Findings in relation to the older children of mothers in the study are particularly striking, interesting and worthy of further study.[15]

Effects on mothers and children

All the mothers felt their 'punishment' would have been more effective if it was a community based punishment, several felt that *'had there been support* earlier', they might *'never have ended up' in prison'*. Mothers talked about the value of women's centres and how they thought they were better equipped to meet their needs than prison.

A few of the mothers described positive aspects of being in prison, two mentioned good medical care and caring staff, one reported *'eating regular meals and having a routine'* as a positive, stating her anxiety was *'reduced'* as a result. Another spoke of being able to access support for domestic abuse, enabling her to make a life changing decision to leave an abusive partner. Two others felt the prison sentence assisted them in becoming *'clean and sober'*. Several mothers spoke warmly of the friendships they had made with each other, some stating their paths would not otherwise have crossed *'outside'*, but now considered women they had met in prison, *'friends for life'*. Mothers spoke of now being more appreciative of their relationships with their children and for some, that because of their absence, their children were closer to their fathers, (for some closer relationships to replacement primary carers was also a negative, as they felt this resulted in distance from them as mothers). However, it is perhaps important to note, without exception these mothers stated, *'it didn't need to be prison' to achieve this'* – with none of them feeling like the prison sentence was more positive than negative. One mother in particular, described her experience as *'traumatic'* and felt she would *'never entirely recover'*. She goes on to say, '*I know that as a family we have all been deeply affected'*. Another wrote, *'prison changes you, and not in a good way'*.

In relation to the children, the mothers described both short and long-term effects on their children (most of our mothers had been out of prison for some time, all but one prior to the changes introduced under the Transforming Rehabilitation (TR) legislation). Several described younger ones as *'clingy' and insecure'*, and conversely older children as *'more independent'*, *'distanced'* or *'aloof'*. Mothers

---

[15] Baldwin's ongoing Doctoral Research *'Motherhood Disrupted: Exploring the Emotional Impact of Imprisonment on Mothers'*, is revealing similar findings described by mothers in relation to older children. De Montfort University, 2014-ongoing. Older children and adult children of imprisoned mothers are also discussed in Baldwin's forthcoming research on grandmothers affected by the CJS.

reported their children experienced, bedwetting, nightmares and anxiety. Older children were described as *'angry'* and *'resentful'*, less amenable to maternal discipline and *'quietly judging'*, and *'as though they were punishing me for leaving them'*. Some children experienced bullying at school because of having a mother in prison. One sibling group were instructed to keep their mother's whereabouts a secret to avoid stigma, for the whole of the mother's five-month prison sentence.

Post release

Four mothers, (Anna, Delia, Debbie and Ethel), were evicted from their homes during their time in prison, another (Jade), has *'eviction pending'*. This devastating consequence of a short sentence was described by Debbie; *'I lost my house and had to start again. I found it impossible because I couldn't get a house because I was under 35 and my 18-month-old daughter wasn't living with me. I hoped that someone would help me with that. But they didn't'*. Anna, highlighting the tautological issue many evicted mothers post release face, wrote, *'being evicted means landlords won't give me a chance and the council don't make a priority because I don't have my kids yet, but I can't get them because I don't have a home. So, I'm stuck.'* For those not evicted, many faced leaving prison to accumulated debt and rent arrears, rendering the women vulnerable to future eviction and/or re offending. Which of course also renders children vulnerable to disruption and homelessness.

Time and again, post release families, especially grandmothers, were reported as the greatest source of support. One mother described her probation officer as extremely helpful, and having supported her with access to work. Others described supervision as *'pointless'*, *'costly'* and *'annoying'*. As previously stated, all bar one mother was released pre-TR and so not subject to the 12-month period of supervision. A larger scale repeat of the study, post TR would be very interesting and illuminating, both in terms of perception of supervision and breach. Women in the study who attended women's' centers as part of their supervision found them incredibly helpful, two women continued to attend long after her release, with one subsequently going on to, initially volunteer at the center, and later become a full-time employee. Interestingly two other mothers expressed the desire to *'use their experience for the good'* and wished to seek work or volunteering with organizations working with women affected by the CJS. Several mothers felt that support they received as a result of their prison sentence, ought to have been available to them sooner. Although grateful for the women's centre, one mother said, *'I'm sad that I had to go to prison to access any support for myself and my children'*.

It was clear that despite fact that these women had spent only short periods in custody, the mothers in the study remained troubled by their experiences. All the mothers described challenges that had carried on for them long after their release. One mother in fact felt she had PTSD, and found herself *'unable to do even the simplest of things, such as post a letter'.*

We conclude the report with recommendations for the future. We echo and reiterate the Prison Reform Trust recommendations about the sentencing of mothers. We highlight the need for mothers to be supported in their mothering role, pre, during and post custody to secure better outcomes for themselves and their children. We acknowledge this will require consistent and permanent funding and investment, which is of paramount importance. We suggest a renewed and invigorated return to the Corston Report and its 43 recommendations, with commitment, matched by investment, to achieve its aims.

We call for a formal process for systematically securing accurate statistics in relation to the *actual* numbers of mothers in custody, the numbers of children affected, and their subsequent whereabouts. We call for recognition and formal support of the temporary primary carers, with an emphasis on research to establish the needs of carers and indeed the children in their care. We suggest a presumption against short sentences and a presumption against sentencing pregnant women; we suggest a number of Mother and Baby Units (MBU's) for vulnerable mothers could and should be located in the community (while incorporating all of the principles of good practice as suggested by Birth Companions[16]). Ideally with consideration also being given to the development and funding of community based residential support for mothers and their children.

We, like many before us, would like to see fewer women sentenced to custody in the first instance, with significant revision of the sentencing framework to achieve this. We urge sentencers to be consistently mindful of EU guidance and the Bangkok rules. We acknowledge that revision of the sentencing framework may be a longer-term goal.

---

[16] Birth Companions is a unique charity which supports women experiencing severe disadvantage during pregnancy, birth and early parenting to overcome the inequalities they face and fulfil their potential in prisons and the community. http://www.birthcompanions.org.uk/

We recommend the development of specific training about the need to factor into sentencing decisions information about primary care responsibilities and the best interests of children,[17] but importantly, we also recommend the urgent development of gender specific sentencing guidelines. We feel that gender specific guidelines are an achievable aim that will facilitate equal and fair treatment, without the uniformity that currently disadvantages women, meaning both their and their children's needs are compromised.

D. Methodology

Data considered for this report is drawn from the completed questionnaires of 17 mothers who had served a period in custody, of shorter than 12 months. The sample comprised mothers, from diverse backgrounds across England and Wales. All the participants had been released from prison for over 12 months, and were no longer subject to license supervision. The 17 participants were mothers to a total of fifty children, aged between 18 months and 19 years old.

The participants were secured via several means. With the permission of stakeholders, posters inviting participants to contribute were placed in several women's centres. Additionally, invitations to contribute to the research were placed in a prison newspaper and prison magazine. Existing professional contacts of the researchers were utilized, leading to a first line of participants, from which, via snowball sampling, additional participants were secured. Several participants contacted one or both researchers directly, stating a willingness to be involved in the research. Some of the participants completed questionnaires independently, returning them to the researchers by post, others completed them either in the researcher's presence or with the researcher asking the questions from the questionnaire, and writing the responses verbatim on the participant's behalf (thereby facilitating the contributions of at least two of the participants who could not easily read and write). All participants contributed to the research voluntarily and signed consent forms. The questionnaire was devised and adapted following consultation with several stakeholders, including Probation, Women in Prison and Women's Breakout[18], and further informed via consultation and a focus group with women who had experienced prison as mothers. The

---

[17] 'We note that the ESRC has funded a project, led by Shona Minson, Oxford University Centre for Criminology, to develop such training materials, also supported by the Prison Reform Trust. https://www.law.ox.ac.uk/centres-institutes/centre-criminology

[18] Women in Prison are a charity which works to support women in all the women's prisons (http://www.womeninprison.org.uk/); Women's Breakout are a national organisation of women's centres who work with women in contact with the criminal justice system (http://womensbreakout.org.uk/

research was ethically approved by Coventry University's faculty ethics committee. The data was analysed thematically.

E. Limitations of the research

We acknowledge that this research covers a small sample of 17 mothers and was gathered via lengthy questionnaires. Therefore, there is an obvious limitation to how far we can draw conclusions from this relatively small sample. Though the findings of this study do indeed support and echo the finding of previous research in this field (Caddle and Crisp 1997, Carlen 2002, Epstein 2012, Minson 2014, Masson 2014, Baldwin 2017). Despite the relatively small participant sample, it is important to note that there was a total of fifty children affected by the imprisonment of their mothers in this study, arguably a significant number. We did not stipulate to the women any specific length of time since their last sentence, therefore many of the participants are reflecting on sentences from some time past, and importantly pre-TR). Therefore, as most of the participants were not subject to statutory supervision, this research may present a different picture from post TR research in relation to post custodial supervision and breach.

Although their views and voice are presented via their mother's narratives, the impact on the children, as described by their mothers, is evident. It is true that the mothers were reflecting on experiences in their past, therefore their reflections may be reliant on memories and subsequent emotions that may have altered over time. However, as Baldwin has previously argued *'whilst reflective post prison accounts might not be as raw as accounts given whilst mothers are still incarcerated, it is possible that the persistence of such powerful memories and emotions, reflects the depth at which they were felt"* (2017:3).

F. Findings

1. Our participants

Seventeen mothers contributed to this study: we stipulated only that the mothers had served sentences of less than 12 months, were no longer subject to formal supervision, and that they were mothers of 'children' of any age. We make a distinction between those who served a sentence because of a criminal offence, 15 women, and those two women who had committed no crime - they were committed to custody for arrears of council tax: their pseudonyms are Clare and Lily. Two solicitors have carefully examined their papers and have given us their opinion that the committal to prison of these two women was an error on the part of the sentencing magistrates and was thus unlawful [19]. (See Table 1 and the Appendix).

i. Ethnicity (See Table 1)

The participants in the study were diverse, most participants did not disclose their ages, but the age range of the children (18 months to 19), gives some indication of the age range of the mothers. In terms of ethnicity, the participants' make up, being self-described as, 47% white British, 17% black British, 17% white Irish, and 6% Welsh, Mixed Race and 'not stated', respectively.

ii. Pre-custodial vulnerabilities (See Table 1)

As might have been expected, this group of 17 women revealed themselves to be vulnerable or facing challenges on many fronts, particularly socio-economically, psychologically and physically. Depression and anxiety were mentioned by 14 mothers (82%). Six reported current or previous addiction issues (35%). In fact, all the mothers described some form of pre-existing vulnerability or difficulty. Three were pregnant at the time of entering prison. Two mothers were widows (Sally and Rose). Only one (Lily) was living with the father of her child; the remaining 16 described themselves as single parents (94%), many were parents of children with additional needs, (one had a disabled child, one reported *'my daughter is dyslexic'*, one wrote that her twins were very premature and had health issues, and another had one child with *'ADHD and learning difficulties'*, another a child with *'challenging behaviour'*. Lily, lives with epilepsy and depression, and had been the victim of a serious assault (on her and her partner). One reported that when she entered prison she was suffering from *'crack-induced psychosis'* (which she felt the prison dealt with well).

Anna, reported complex and multiple needs, physical health and mental health issues, substance abuse. Betty reported: *'I was drinking a lot and I had bad nerves. I never self-harmed but my daughter does.'*

Cassy was depressed, and on medication on reception into prison, she reported that her panic attacks began in prison, she had made a suicide attempt before prison, she also had a history of self-harm. Cassy was under the care of a Community Psychiatric Nurse before going to prison, and post-prison. Clare, a survivor of domestic abuse, was living with PTSD. Debbie reported alcoholism,

---

[19] We thank solicitors Clementine Harrison and Samuel Genen for their help in this regard.

mental health issues, depression, and misuse of drugs. Ethel suffered from depression and anxiety, had a history of self-harm, anxiety and substance misuse. Sandra reported depression, anxiety, addiction, self-harm and cannabis use. Mandy had panic attacks which she also reported started in prison, she also self-harmed in prison, *'for the first time in a long time'*. Delia had substance misuse issues, including drug induced psychosis. She reported: *'I had severe substance abuse problems, I was losing the ability to function and losing the ability to be a mother.'*

Michelle had a history of depression, and described feeling suicidal in prison. Melissa was diabetic. Jade suffered depression and had self-harmed. Jenna reported depression and panic attacks as did Ethel. Sandra's first child was born when Sandra was only 13 years old following a *'traumatic childhood.'* Sandra suffers from depression and anxiety, she has self-harmed in the past, and has used cannabis *'to calm my nerves ... I used to be a big drinker but I'm not now as my liver is damaged. I have some pills for my liver and some anti-depressants'*. Melissa also disclosed experiencing domestic violence, she reported: *'My partner assaulted me regularly''*. Rose disclosed that she felt problems associated with grief, the menopause and mental health issues played a role in her offending. Only one mother (Clare) reported no physical or mental health problems.

2. Background to Offending and Sentencing

i. Poverty

In some cases, the mothers reported that their offending was directly related to issues of poverty. Polly was sentenced for tampering with the electricity meter. She reported: *'My benefit was frozen because of a stupid mistake. I just couldn't manage. I didn't even have enough money to heat my house.'* Sally committed fraud, using a catalogue in a friend's name, to order Christmas presents for her children. She stated:

> *'I don't think judges even think about our families when they sentence us - they say we should thinking about kids when we offend – well I was – I committed fraud to order Christmas presents for my kids. I knew it was wrong, but I couldn't bear for them to have nothing'*.

Perhaps the most shocking example linked to poverty of all was Debbie, who was sentenced to custody for shoplifting: she stole baby milk, baby bottles and nappies. Debbie highlighted, what for her is an anomaly of the 'system'. She stated; *'All that money spent on courts, legal aid and prison – Yet I couldn't afford nappies and food. It doesn't make sense'.* Debbie goes on to say:

> *Sometimes I just want someone to help me make my head peaceful, try living on benefits, not knowing if the money would last, which it doesn't. Loans got me through, but I just got deeper into debt, they stopped loaning because I couldn't pay. I've pawned everything I've ever owned…. I just think how do you survive with addictions, depression, anxiety, not knowing how you will heat the house or put electric on.*

Rose, who was a widow, was subject to a debt management plan at the time of her offending. Another mother stated *'capping benefits and the bedroom tax has forced people into crime. Truly'.* Michelle reported:

> I *was struggling, really struggling to pay my bills – there needs to be more support for single mums. I knew loads of mums in prison who were just trying to find ways to manage.*

ii. Addiction

Some mothers (35%), reported addiction played a major role in current or previous offending, and in the breach of court-imposed conditions (see below). For example, Betty's offence was a public order offence, *'drunk in the shops'.* She stated the background to her drinking related to her difficulty managing her stress and emotions following an assault on her daughter, reporting that:

> *'I was drunk because my daughter – the eldest one – told me she had been raped by my boyfriend and I felt sick. He was arrested, but they don't know if they will prosecute they said, and I was scared of him and what he would do. I felt bad for letting down my daughter and couldn't cope. I'm OK now and he went to jail in the end. My daughter is OK now too.'*

Debbie described her addiction and her poverty:

> *Sometimes I just think – how do you survive with addictions, depression, anxiety, not knowing how you will heat the house or put electric on? I had a hard life, my dad was horrible to us, he hurt us and my mum. I had a teacher at school that wanted to help, but he was as bad. I had kids and I couldn't look after them*

> *because no one helped. I hated my dad but when he died I thought it would be better, but it wasn't for me, it just made me drink more. My kids suffered. Sometimes I just want someone to help me make my head peaceful. Try living on benefits, with the stresses of not knowing if the money would last, which it doesn't. Provident Loans made me poorer, they got me through but I just got deeper in debt, they stopped loaning because I couldn't pay. I've pawned everything I ever owned. It doesn't get easier.*

iii. Sentencers' consideration of participants as mothers

Several mothers in the study felt their circumstances as mothers of dependent children, were not given any consideration by the court, Lily for example, stated she felt she didn't have the opportunity to talk about her family in court, despite her being her partner's main carer as well as being a mother of a dependent child. Lily stated her solicitor told her *'the judge isn't interested in sob stories'*. Another mother told us *I don't think the judges even think about our families when they sentence us'*. Mandy, who was placed on remand, told us of her experience in court as she was remanded:

> *'they did not take into account my circumstances, I even told the court I had my son at school who didn't know where I was – they said they would let me ring a relative or phone social services, there was no regard for how this might affect my son – none.'*

One mother, Delia, described how, once it became apparent during her hearing that custody was likely, she absconded from the court in order that she could make childcare arrangements for her children before she was *'sent down'*:

> *I knew I was going to be given a custodial sentence, so I absconded from court to sort out childcare. I then had to hand myself in once childcare was sorted. Very few judges pay close attention to the needs of the family.*

Several mothers commented on the expense of prosecuting them via the courts for low level offending, when in their view *'there are other ways to punish'*, or *'sorting out the issues that led me to offend in the first place'*, being *'better'* use of public funds. Particularly when, as was the view of the majority, *'prison achieved nothing'.*

iv. Offences (See Table 1)

None of the mothers in this research had committed offences involving violence. Two of our mothers had not committed any criminal offence: (this is covered more fully in the Appendix). They were sent to prison for council tax debt. Solicitors who have since examined the papers have given us their view that both these committals were a result of error on the part of the magistrates and were unlawful. Of the other 15, 4 were sentenced for shoplifting. Of these one was sentenced for both benefit fraud and shoplifting. Two were sentenced for public disorder offences, being drunk in public. Ethel's offences were theft and criminal damage, she damaged a vending machine. Polly: theft from electricity meter. Sandra: shoplifting and possession of cannabis. Sally committed fraud and Rose committed theft from her employer. For five of the imprisoned mothers this was their first offence (29%).

v. Sentences served

The longest sentence served in this group was 34 weeks (Debbie); the shortest was 2 weeks (Lily); the average was 12 weeks. Although some had previously been remanded, only one of the participant's most recent period of custody was as a remand prisoner. Mandy, had not been expecting to be remanded (or indeed, like several mothers in the study, sentenced to custody). Mandy was pregnant and the mother of a four-year-old boy when she was sentenced to 5 months, for receiving stolen goods. When asked if she was expecting a custodial sentence, she reported:

No, I was shocked and so was my legal. I really didn't think I would get sentenced to custody…but then neither did I expect to be remanded. When that happened, my son was at school, obvs I hadn't told him where I was – you don't discuss things like that with a four-year-old, so he knew nothing. Luckily on the morning of court I'd said to my mum " if I don't ring you by 2 they've took me down'. I only said it in jest and we didn't think it would really happen. If I hadn't of said that she wouldn't even have known to go and get my son from pre-school. I suppose I should have considered it, but I hadn't been in trouble for years and it wasn't a dead serious offence or nothing.

Another mother, Delia, had served 8 previous sentences, all of 12 weeks or less, and including a remand period of three weeks when she was eight and a half months pregnant, her child was born six days after she was released.

In the study, the mothers' most recent or only sentence was as follows; Clare, 7 weeks; Lily, 2 weeks. Anna, 13 weeks; Betty, 9 weeks; Cassey, 13 weeks; Debbie, 23 weeks; Delia 12 weeks; Ethel, 21 weeks; Jade, 9 weeks; Jenna, 17 weeks; Mandy, 9 weeks; Melissa, 4 weeks; Michelle, 9 weeks; Polly, 14 weeks; Sandra, 13 weeks; Sally, 16 weeks; Rose 26 and a half weeks.

vi. Breach of conditions imposed by a court

Although none of the participants reported that their most recent offence was breach, Anna had a breach hearing pending and three other mothers had previously breached their orders. Delia reported:

> '*My substance abuse was out of control, I could just about get out of bed in the mornings and when I did it was to feed myself drugs.... My offence was failing to appear before court even though I called the court on the morning to explain my circumstances of my benefits not being paid on the day so I had no means of travel.*'

Asked why she was remanded in custody and not given bail, and was this explained to her in court, she replied: '*Yes, it was explained but they did not take into account my circumstances.*' The mothers who had breached previous orders or not paid previous fines reported financial hardship as the most relevant factor. Anna explained that she was breached because of '*different kids' birthdays & travelling for visits to one of the kid's dad in prison*'. She had been unable to pay her fines or afford the travel to her supervision appointments, resulting in the breach. Similarly, Jenna reported that '*missed appointments*' had been the reason for her breach, with again financial hardship given as her reason for failing to attend.

3. Health and Wellbeing

i. How did being in prison affect health

As discussed above our sample of 17 women reported several pre-existing and ongoing, physical and mental health challenges and issues (see Table 1). The mothers in the study who had depression and anxiety issues reported the most significant impact, in terms of their mental health. Of the two mothers who reported physical health issues (pregnancy is addressed separately), i.e.

diabetes and epilepsy, one reported a delay in medication and the other *'no issues'.*

Sally described feeling, *'the worst'* she'd ever felt, but praised the healthcare staff for how they had responded to her. Jenna felt that prison made her depression and anxiety worse, as too did Sandra. Jenna expressed the desire to complete a course that she felt would have assisted her anxiety management, but it was not possible due to the length of her sentence. Cassy told us she suffers from panic attacks, which started when she was in prison. Rose, who was facing physical challenges related to the menopause, was refused HRT in prison, she stated:

> *Well for a time I think it made my mental health worse, especially while I was waiting for my tablets- as for the 'lady stuff', well I think that would have been bad out or in, but I think it would have been easier to manage if I was at home.*

Lily, imprisoned for council tax debt (see appendix), describes herself as *'traumatised'* from her time in custody, she is now receiving counselling and feels her time in prison has deeply affected her mental health; which, as she also suffers from epilepsy, impacts on her physical health too. Lily did not receive her epilepsy medication for five days after her arrival in prison, something which she stated added to her stress and anxiety.

Michelle who discovered she was pregnant on reception into custody said she felt *'stressed'* all the time, blaming that stress for the subsequent loss of her baby whilst in custody. Polly also miscarried in prison, something she blamed on the *'shock'* of going to prison' (see below).

In contrast to the experiences described above are two more positive accounts. Delia felt that her mental health improved whilst she was in prison, as she was able to access the prison inreach mental health team. Ethel, felt she benefitted from *'regular meals'*.

ii. Medication in prison

Most of the mothers, who had pre-existing physical or mental health issues, reported problems with accessing health care and receiving medication while they were in prison, mainly on reception into custody. **All** the mothers who had reported they were *'depressed'* and on medication prior to entering prison, experienced delays in having their medication supplied. Rose reported one of the longest delays in receiving medication: she waited 10 days before getting her anti-depressants, the actual longest reported was three and a half weeks. Most stated a delay of around 7 days.

Lily, who suffers from epilepsy and depression, was not given any medication for five days. Cassy, who suffers from depression and who had previously attempted suicide, and who has help from a Community Psychiatric Nurse (CPN), reported '*It took ages to get my tablets'*. Sandra too who suffers from depression and anxiety and who was pregnant at the time reported '*It took 'forever'* to get tablets sorted. Sally reported:

> It took nearly a week to get my tablets, that was hard, especially as I was the lowest I've ever felt. I was suicidal being away from my kids.

Sandra, who also experienced a delay stated; '*my depression was worse than ever, and that was when my self-harm was at its worst. I was anxious all of the time and worried about the kids'*.

Ethel said that she '*got no help'* for her anxiety while she was in prison. When asked if her anxiety issues were addressed, Ethel stated '*I wouldn't say they were addressed. I was asked when I went in, I told them I had anxiety- they asked if I was suicidal, I said I wasn't – and that was that.'* Debbie wrote that she couldn't get regular medications; '*I was on anti-depressants and sleepers before I went in, but I couldn't get regular meds and so it was just worse'*. Michelle reported:

> '*It took over a week to get my medication – I thought this was dreadful and I had withdrawals and felt really unwell – I was almost suicidal – which sounds dramatic now but I remember feeling like it was the beginning of the end for me – I couldn't see how me or the kids would ever get over my being away.'*

Rose reported:

> '*There was no understanding at all of my change [menopause] issues. Outside my GP was going to put me on HRT, which I was desperate for, but the one in prison said I was too young and wouldn't consider it".* Rose wrote: '*Prison made my mental health worse, especially while I was waiting for my tablets.'*

Two of our 17 participants (11%), reported *'good'* medical care in prison. Mandy, who was pregnant and said the staff were good - she saw a nurse straightaway. Delia reported that she entered prison suffering from crack-induced psychosis and that the prison care was excellent; she was successfully treated and felt *'cared for'.*

iii. Pregnancy and miscarriage

Three of the participants were pregnant on entering prison. Mandy reported *'no difficulties'*; she stated staff were *'very good'*, and that she asked for, and was given a chance to see a nurse immediately. She further stated, *'actually all of the prison staff were very good to me'.* For the remaining two, the outcomes were very different. Both Michelle and Polly miscarried in prison. Polly was four months pregnant when she entered prison, telling us:

> *'I was pregnant and had had two episodes of spotting – which they knew and they still put me on my own. I wanted to see a midwife and I was told I couldn't. I'd have to see the nurse. I was upset and wanted to ask loads of questions but I never got to ask them because I lost the baby anyway. I think it was the shock of going to prison that made me lose my baby. I had no history of miscarriage, there was no other reason'. 'When I lost my baby, I was bleeding on my own in my cell for hours. I was terrified, and the prison said they would get me to the doctors in the morning. I was in so much pain they called an ambulance eventually. I lost my baby on the way to the hospital, in handcuffs. I will never forgive them for that. There was no need for cuffs. I wasn't exactly running away, was I?'*

It is worth recalling here that Polly was sentenced to 6 months in prison for interfering with her electricity meter. Both mothers who miscarried, felt that the stress of their imprisonment had a direct impact on the outcome of their pregnancies. Michelle reported:

> *'I lost the baby in prison and I will always believe that was down to the stress of being locked up – I'm certain I would have carried that baby if I'd been out – I still struggle with the guilt of it – I feel like I've killed my baby by getting sent to prison – I've had to have counselling to deal with it.'*

Two of the pregnant mothers stated they did not think pregnant women should be sent to prison, with one stating *'it's not safe and it's not right'.* Sandra, who was in the very early stages of pregnancy, reported no pregnancy related issues.

4. Children

i. How many, with mother or in care

These 17 mothers had between them, 50 children. All the mothers had at least one dependent child living at home at the point of sentence. In total 9 were either in care at point of sentence, or were placed in care because of their mother's sentence. Forty-one, so 82%, of the participants' children, were living with their mothers at the point of sentence. They ranged in age from 18 months to 19 years of age.

ii. Children, needs, health problems, vulnerabilities

Many of the participants' children, suffered from health problems and had other vulnerabilities, see Table 1. Sally's 14-year-old has ADHD and behaviour issues. Lily's 16-year-old daughter for example suffered from such severe anxiety that she had been unable to attend school for the past two years. Michelle's two-year-old twins had been born prematurely and had health issues. Debbie's three eldest children, now in care, were born with Foetal Alcohol Syndrome (FAS), however she remained the primary carer for her 18-month-old child. Sandra's eldest child, age 16, also had FAS. Betty's daughter, age 17, self-harmed, and her youngest child, age 4, is disabled. Jenna's 6-year-old lived with her but had spent time in care as a baby.

iii. Care of children while mother was in prison

Unusually, in comparison with more consistently recorded statistics in this area, five (29%), of the mothers' children's fathers were either the main or shared carer during their mother's sentence. The more commonly reported figure is 9% (Prison Reform Trust 2015). In several cases the children were split up, sometimes across multiple residences. Jade's children for example, were separated, the father had the eldest child, her mother had the two younger children. Michelle's children too were split up; her twins were at home with their father, her daughter went to her father. Sandra's children were also split, the 2 youngest being with their father. Similarly, Sandra's' children were cared for by two separate paternal grandmothers and one father. In 7 cases (41%), mothers or mothers in law of the participants, had the care of the children. The participants' sisters took care of the children in two cases. Delia's children were only briefly looked after by her sister, then entered the care system as 'she couldn't cope'. In only three cases were the children able to stay in their own home, with the father being the carer in two of these instances, and the children's grandmother in the other case.

iv. Did prison ask about children?

Six of our sample (35%), said that the prison knew they had children, either they were asked or they told the prison they had children. Delia answered: '*I told the prison but they showed very little interest.*' Michelle too wrote: '*The prison knew but didn't really seem bothered.*' The exception was Mandy: '*The prison knew I had a son and were really good about it*'. Sally said she wasn't asked but it came up in conversation. Rose said she was asked and replied that her children were all '*grown up*' (which wasn't the case), as she did not want to reveal information about her children. Ethel stated she was asked if she had children, but no further questions. Sandra, a mother of 5, reported she wasn't asked, which she felt was because she 'looked so young', that the assumption was made that she did not have children. However, she went on to say that once aware the prison family engagement worker (FEW), then made enquiries and 'checked on them all'. Mandy said,' *the prison knew I had a son and were really good about it'.* Three mothers reported actively avoiding talking to prison staff about their children, concerned doing so would lead to intervention of some sort. Rose gave her reason as '*I didn't want anyone poking in our business'.*

Some of the mothers commented that they were asked when they were received into custody, but that children or their whereabouts, were 'not *brought up again'.* Several mothers reported that the PACT workers and the FEW enquired about their children and offered assistance.

v. Worries about children

The participants revealed severe stress, anxiety and worry about the children they left behind when they entered prison. Ethel reported that her child was bullied because of the mother's custody. Her children stayed with their father and although Ethel '*knew*' they would be OK '*but you still worry as the mum, don't you?*' Polly too reported that her 7-year-old child got bullied. Sandra expressed her upset that her children were split up; she was worried that the children would forget each other, '*and not be as close as they were'.* Her daughter age 16 got pregnant while her mother was in prison. Michelle said:

> '*I know it wasn't really long in the grand scheme of things but it felt like it at the time. When you've never really left your kids before to be away from them 24/7 is just awful.*'

She went on to say she felt *'stressed and unhappy'* that the kids had to be split up *'I was worried all the time about how they would feel about each other'* when *I'm released'.* She worried about how the father of the 2-year-old twins would cope, telling us: *'I was worried all the time he would drink when he was with them. It was very stressful and I tried not to think about it most of the time, but it's impossible when you're a mum to switch off'.* Jenna said, *'I was terrified that social service would take her again'* (child is 6). Lily reported: *'I was very worried. Louise comes to me with her anxiety issues, I'm the one who helps her cope. I am the one she turns to for everything, I'm the one that gives her the reassurance she seeks'.*

For many the worry continued after their imprisonment ended. Michelle, whose children were looked after by their fathers, one of whom had alcohol issues, reported:

> *'I worry about what went on when I was away. It tortures me in fact, but I'll never really know that they were properly looked after in that time.'* Another mother wrote that she was worried *'my daughter would start her periods and I wouldn't be there.'*

vi. Impact on older children

A significant finding of this research was the impact of the mother's sentence on their older children. Melissa, Sally and Rose had daughters aged 17-19 who cared for their younger siblings while their mother was in prison. For two of the daughters, this had meant disrupting their full-time education, one was not sure if she would return to education at the time of reporting. Melissa's daughter was responsible for her siblings aged 11 and 15; Rose's daughter was left in charge of children of 12 and 10, Sally's eldest child looked after children age 14, 12 and 4, with some help from members of the family, and help with cooking. In addition, some older children were in fact left apparently without formal care arrangements or supervision. Clare's eldest child (17), did not experience formal care arrangements, instead, *'stayed with friends'.* Betty's eldest, also 17, *'came and went'.*

Mothers described how their older children particularly were *'angry'* or *'embarrassed'.* Ethel reported that her oldest child refuses to talk about their experience and that she was bullied for having a mother in prison, Ethel feels her daughter is ashamed of her. She feels that her daughter became more *'independent'* whilst she was *'away'*, and that this continues to cause conflict between them.

5. Visits and contact

i. Seeing/contact with children

All the mothers maintained telephone contact with their children, although this was not without its issues. Mothers struggled to afford the phone regularly, particularly when children were separated across more than one home, (which was the case in 29% of the families). Mothers effectively had to 'choose' which child to ring when funds were low. Michelle, whose children (twins aged 2, daughter 3) were separated across two homes, stated:

> *Phoning was hard because they were in separate houses, I felt guilty if phoned the twins and not Sinead. I felt she needed me more (because she was older) so then id ring her, but felt guilty about the twins.*

Several mothers again described how PACT were instrumental in assisting them with maintaining at least postal contact with their children[20], sometimes allowing phone calls to be made from the PACT offices in particular circumstances, for example when one child was experiencing bullying at school, the PACT team allowed the mother to ring the school to discuss the situation. The mother felt this was helpful, inclusive and reassuring. Several mothers described a delay in being able to make the first phone calls to their children, on more than one occasion, up to a week.

Michelle, one mother who experienced this delay related how for her this was both painful and frustrating:

> *It took a few days when I first went in. I think it was over a week, but I can't remember now – I've blocked that week out I think. However long it was, I know it was the longest I'd ever gone without speaking to them, and that's not right is it? When you have gone away and they don't have a clue why, that's when you need to speak to them the most ...but the prison didn't care.*

With one exception, the mothers in our group saw their children at least once during their imprisonment: only one, Sandra did not see her children. She lives in

---

[20] PACT provides at least one pre-paid letter home for mothers per week.

Wales, there is no female prison in Wales; she was in England, about 100 miles from her home. For her the distance and costs were prohibitive. The distance made it impossible for her children to see her. Asked 'How did you find prison visits with your children?', she replied: 'I *wish I could tell you!*' She felt her youngest, who was 3 months old when she was sentenced, 'forgot' her. She wrote:

> *It broke my heart it did. I knew the baby would forget me completely and she did. When I got her back, I felt like she wasn't even mine. She wanted her nana, and cried coming to me.*

The other mothers all had visits; although 7 (41%) had only one visit; Ethel's children visited twice; Mandy's child visited every week. Another mother from Wales had one visit, but that was only possible because of PACT, who arranged and facilitated the visit, *'if it wasn't for PACT I wouldn't have seen them at all'.*

ii. What were the reasons for lack of visits?

Most of the participants (59%), reported distance and /or the costs of travelling to prison as a factor in not receiving regular visits. Although there is a government scheme[21], only one participant mentioned applying for assistance, though also reported quickly abandoning this as *'too complicated'*. No other participants mentioned applying for help from this scheme.

Lily wrote visiting prison was *'costly'*, Anna said to bring children to see her was *'too hard, and too dear,'* Betty too wrote it was *'too dear'*, and Delia and Polly made the same comment *'it was too costly'*. Sally said it was *'too far, too expensive and the children would have had to take time off school'*. Rose had visits from her children every other week. Some of the mothers felt that the visits were *'too difficult'* emotionally for both them and their children, with several deciding *'to protect'* their children (and sometimes themselves) from the pain of visits. Others made the decision not to repeat the visit because of journey difficulties in terms of the afore mentioned distance or cost, or both.

---

[21] The Assisted Prison Visits Unit, to which people can apply for help with travel costs for visiting a close relative or partner in prison (**Assisted Prison Visits Unit** assisted.prison.visits@noms.gsi.gov.uk

iii. How were the visits for the mother, and for the children?

Two reported that *'it was OK'*. For others, the experience was difficult. Ethel wrote that coming to see her in prison was boring for the children *'the two older children hated visits'*, because they were *'embarrassed'*. Jenna said visits were *'too stressful'*; Polly wrote *'Visits were painful'*.

Anna's children visited only once; distance to prison and cost of visits were problems. She told us:

> *'My family wanted to bring my kids but it was too far. My sister tried to get help but it just didn't happen, she said it was too complicated'*. *'I couldn't cope with seeing them, and it was too expensive anyway'*. *'They were difficult to contact, I didn't have much funds, no letters'*.

Betty had one visit only, distance and cost were issues, telephone calls expensive so limited phone contact, she sent some letters. Cassy who was in a local prison had visits from her children once a month, and phoned every other night. Debbie says she didn't see her children while she was in prison because her mother wouldn't bring them, so contact was by phone. Home is on Isle of Wight so the grandmother would not make the journey. Ethel said children found the visits boring; journey to prison was long, hard and expensive so they only came twice.

Jenna's home was in also in Wales. The journey to the prison was over 100 miles. PACT arranged a visit, but only once was possible. Mandy, who was in a local prison, says visits did not cause problems, she saw her children weekly *'It was OK we told them it was Mummy's work'*. Her 4-year-old did not really understand, he wasn't fazed by it at all, but she (mother) got really upset when he left. Although the visits went well Mandy reported how visiting had had a permanent impact on her son, *'He didn't like the dogs. He is still scared of dogs'*. One other mother stated her children had also found the dogs, *'scary'*. Delia said the distance to prison was a problem; it took 5 months before a visit took place and even then, only 2 children came because *'social services failed to make arrangements'*. She said the visit was *'very strange and uncomfortable and false but at the same time very overwhelming and we had a happy visit for what it was'*.

Michelle: who was in prison 70 miles from home; only saw the twins, age 2, the oldest child (age 3) did not see her. She said:

> 'It was really awful, they cried, I cried, they didn't understand what was happening it was just stressful. I wasn't supposed to put them on my knee, but how do you explain that to two two-year-olds, so I just kept letting them up, but all the time I was terrified the visit would be ended. I spent the whole visit stressed and in knots. Even if they could have come back, I don't think I would have wanted it. It was too much'.

Polly's mother brought the children to see her in prison. '*I often used to think it would have been easier not to see them.*' She found the prison visits painful. '*One visit got cancelled due to lock-up and that was traumatic for us all*'. Melissa's eldest child brought the two younger ones to prison. There was only one visit. She didn't want them to visit again. Jade's children had one visit. The children were with grandmother who didn't want them to remember that they had been in a prison, she brought them only once. Jade said:

> It was awful anyway. I wasn't allowed out of my seat. I wasn't allowed them on my knee. It's cruel, why punish them if it's me that's done wrong.

Lily's daughter came with her father to see her. Lily reported: '*It was nice to be able to see her, I had to pretend to her that I was coping. I felt physically sick when we had to say goodbye*'. Michelle, mother of a three-year-old and 2-year-old twins, reported of a prison visit: '*They were crying and confused – they screamed when they left, it was horrible, just horrible*'.

Sally found the one visit her children made 'heart-breaking'. '*They all cried from beginning to end*' (her children were 4, 12, 14 and 17). Her youngest was also upset that she couldn't sit on her mother's knee. Sally described her daughter's upset:

> Even when I explained why, my daughter said, "But Mummy I wouldn't do anything naughty, I promise, shall I go and ask." That broke my heart that did. It made me feel they don't even trust children.

Rose wrote: '*It's hard when you have more than one [child], you have to try to give them all attention. I think my oldest came off worst as she would let the little ones have more time.*'

6. The prison experience

i. How did these mothers experience prison overall, negative and positive aspects

The completed questionnaires painted a picture of great distress in terms of the separation from their children. However, the mothers' responses were not completely devoid of positive statements. Positives were reported in relation to the prison experience, and related to 'benefits' these mothers had extracted from their experiences. Sometimes it appeared these 'extracted positives' originated from an attempt to 'make the best of it', but the mothers themselves described some positives that came directly from their prison experiences, at least one that was potentially life changing (Melissa), and so it is important to record these. Although it must be stated that overall, the reflections were more negatively loaded.

a. Positive aspects

For some of our group there were positive aspects to being in prison. Melissa wrote about receiving help in prison concerning domestic abuse:

> *'I was able to speak to someone about the domestic abuse I had been experiencing. It helped to see I don't need to put up with it. So, I was able to leave my ex behind and not come out to him. I learned I am worth something.*

Cassy said she made some good friends: '*I quite liked prison, I had good mates*'. Ethel said that she ate regular meals and enjoyed the security of prison life which reduced her anxiety. '*I made some friends who will be friends for life. I wouldn't have met them anywhere else as we have nothing in common but where we were. Prison taught me compassion and to judge people less*'.

Sandra said the positive was that she stayed off cannabis, and that her children became closer to their dads. Delia reported positive effect on her health: serious substance abuse problems were well treated in prison. Clare wrote: '*I met people I would never met and made the best of a bad situation, but there are/were no positives or lessons learnt other than how WRONG they were to send me to jail'*. Michelle said the only good thing was that her children became closer to their fathers.

For Rose a positive was that it re-affirmed to her how strong they were as a family, and it made her appreciative of her family and their home circumstances.

'In some ways it brought us closer, but with a shadow over us, if that makes sense'. She now wants to volunteer to help women in prison. Sally reported that she felt that her trauma as a widow was *'put into perspective,'* she felt most of the women in prison *'had been through worse experiences, and for the whole of their lives'.*

b. Negative aspects

The pain of being separated from children, and worry about and for them, features consistently in the descriptions of the mothers.

Clare and Lily, in prison for council tax debt, felt strongly that they did not deserve to be in a prison. Clare wrote:

> *My family and friends and myself still struggle to come to terms with the fact that I was sent to jail. Anyone who knows me thinks I'm joking when I tell them they simply can't believe the injustice.'* For her there was nothing positive about the experience of imprisonment: *'I met people I would never had met and made the best of a bad situation, but there are/were NO positives or lessons learnt other than how WRONG they were to send me to jail.* [emphasis Clare's own].

Lily, too wrote in strongly negative terms about her experience:

> *'I know that as a family, we have all been deeply affected. ... The moment I was sentenced was extremely distressing for us both. He saw me through the doors and he said I collapsed. This is something we are finding very difficult to get out of our head. We weren't allowed to see each other before I was taken away and he was left to tell my daughter when he got home. The whole time I was inside I honestly had physical pain – being torn away from them both. I felt as if I was dead and watching them both struggling to cope without me. ... I don't think I can begin to describe how I felt inside, it was torture, all I wanted was to be back with my family. I felt as though my heart had been torn out.'*

Sally reported: *'Prison changes you and not in a good way. I still feel so angry I was sent to prison.'*

Mandy wrote:

> *'I don't think pregnant women should go to prison – it's not safe and it's not right*

> *– there should be something else – but for my sentence, I should have got a fine or unpaid work.'*

Rose said she felt ashamed, guilty and embarrassed at being in prison. She was sad that her daughter (who cared for the younger children) had to *'grow up so fast,'* by becoming her siblings' carer in her mother's absence.

All bar one mother described some negative consequences as a result of their sentence, and where they had identified positives they did not feel this outweighed the overall negativity of their experiences.

ii. What do the mothers say they 'learned' in prison, if anything

Two participants responded to this question by commenting on the easy availability of drugs while in prison. One stated simply, *'I learned how easy it was to get drugs'.* Mandy said:

> *'The girls I saw prison just made them worse – they either learned how to commit better crime or got addicted to drugs so that they could cope – most of them went out worse than when they went in.'* Jade wrote: *'I learned how easy it is to get drugs and how hard it is to resist them when all you want to do is forget where you are'.*

Anna said she *'learnt how strong we are as a family unit. We managed, we didn't fall out, we did ok'.*

Debbie reported: *'I did a parenting course'.* She said she didn't feel she needed this course, but it was only one she was able to attend in the timescale she was in custody. Two mothers reported there were courses that may have been useful to them, but they had insufficient time to complete the programmes.

Clare said*: 'I've learned that our court system is being used for the wrong reasons.'.* Ethel stated, *'I do now know my weekly safe limit for alcohol and that I'm usually over* it'.

Sally, when asked if she had learned anything, stated:

> *'I've learned that we have a stupid system that spends thousands locking people up instead of spending it on stopping people going to prison in the first place.*

> *I've also learned that cutting benefits and the bedroom tax has forced people into crime.*

Several mothers were very keen to state that they would never go back to prison, but were clear this that wasn't due to anything the *'system did for me '*, but the separation from their children had been so painful that they *'couldn't go through it or put them through it again'.*

iii. Do they believe having been in prison will help to stop future offending?

Clare and Lily felt this question was not relevant to them, as both were sentenced for a civil debt (council tax) and therefore had committed no crime.

Ethel reported: *'Being away from my kids broke my heart. So, in a way, yes, but I don't think it had to be that way – if I'd had more help before I wouldn't have offended in the first place.'* Asked *'Will being in prison stop you getting into trouble again?* Sandra replied*:*

> *Yes and no; I don't ever want to be separated from my kids, so I won't be, but it's not prison that taught me that, if you see what I mean. I just made that decision for me and for them. Prison did nothing but make me feel like a terrible person; it that's what I want to avoid, not prison itself. What would help would be more support before ever going to prison and more understanding about addiction and depression.*

None of the mothers felt prison per se would stop them offending. Two mothers felt it was *more* likely to make them offend again because they felt they had come out to a *'worse situation'* than the one they were in when they were sentenced.

iv. In their view was imprisonment 'fair'?

Both Clare and Lily were clear that sentencing them to prison for not paying council tax was wrong and unfair in their view. Clare wrote: *'I have never committed a crime, therefore to send me to prison was a horrific injustice.'* She further stated *'It was absolutely not fair. I have learned that our court system is being used for the wrong reasons. I have never knowingly offended'*. Lily wrote: *No*, in answer to 'Do you think your imprisonment was fair?'

Mandy, who served 9 weeks for 'handling stolen goods', in reply to the question, 'Do you think your imprisonment was fair' replied '*Not one bit – I only agreed to keep some stuff in my house for a mate – I really didn't ever consider I would go to prison for that, and I still think it was horrific that it happened – especially as I was pregnant.*' Debbie said she didn't think it was fair, and strongly felt it was not fair for her children. She had stolen nappies and baby formula. Debbie wrote:

> '*No, [it's not fair] not for my kids. I needed what I took, I know it's wrong, but what do you do when you need formula and nappies and you don't have money? I only ever took what I needed. You spend all that money on courts and legal costs and prison yet I couldn't afford nappies and food. It doesn't make sense. Sometimes I just think how do you survive with addictions, depression and anxiety not knowing how you will heat the house or put electric on. Sort out problems that cause addiction and give ex-cons a chance.*

Ethel wrote that she didn't think her imprisonment was fair. '*I think it would have been more fair to send me to a centre where I could have either worked a punishment or got help with my issues – I didn't know – but I really think that for what I did it wasn't fair to punish my children. We will never be the same*'.

Sandra said, '*I know I did wrong but I didn't deserve to be punished forever and neither do my kids.*' Sandra thought her imprisonment was not fair, she wrote:

> *No. My brother burgled someone's house and he got unpaid work. I shoplifted and got prison, it made no sense. I would have paid a fine or done unpaid work but it was never even discussed as an option. The judge said I was paying one fine so it would cause me hardship to pay another on top. Well what does he think prison caused me!!*

Michelle said:

> '*No, I don't, I don't think my circumstances were taken into account at all, I was struggling, really struggling to pay my bills. There needs to be more support for single mums. I know loads of mums in prison who were just trying to manage – I know it was wrong what I did, but I don't think I deserved prison. It was traumatic and awful and it took my baby* (reference to miscarriage which occurred in prison.)

When asked, 'Will prison stop you re-offending,' she replied '*Yes and no; I'd never do anything to risk being away from the kids ever again. But I still think it was wrong. If there'd been more support then I wouldn't have gone in in the first place*'.

Michelle, the mother of 3 very young children, imprisoned for benefit fraud, asked do you think your imprisonment was fair, wrote: '*No, I don't – I don't think my circumstances were taken into account at all – I was struggling, really struggling to pay my bills – there needs to be more support for single mums. I knew loads of mums in prison who were just trying to find ways to manage*

Sally, when asked if her imprisonment was fair, replied: *No, not one bit. It was my first offence; unpaid work would have been justified and more appropriate'.* Rose said it was '*a hard question to answer'* because, '*I know I did wrong and deserve to be punished. But I do think a suspended sentence would have been appropriate, but maybe they would have felt that that was like me getting away with it.*'

7. The effects of separation and maternal imprisonment on children

Both short-term and long-term effects on children of their mother being in prison were noted by the mothers. The problems ranged from bed-wetting, being '*whiny*', '*clingy*' '*insecure*', 'difficult to discipline', and some describing the children feeling '*very anxious and needy*'. Sandra, believes that her 16-year-old daughter was not adequately cared for or supervised during her incarceration and, as a result, became pregnant. The baby was adopted.

Both Clare and Lily, who went to prison for council tax debt reported their children having been badly affected. Clare wrote: '*My children have been affected by me having to leave them. They have never been without me. I have never committed a crime, therefore to send me to prison was a horrific injustice. It's made myself and my children very vulnerable, and scared that I may leave them again.*'

Lily, whose family was particularly vulnerable due to the illnesses of both parents, described the serious effects on her daughter from her mother's imprisonment. Lily's daughter suffered from great anxiety and insecurity during her mother's period in prison: Lily told us:

> *Louise was unusually quiet when I was in prison. She usually spends a lot of time in her boyfriend's house and isn't worried about being away from home, but she stayed with her dad always. She kept asking him if he thought I would be OK in*

> *prison, she wanted to know how I was when I was actually sent down. Constantly seeking reassurance that I would be OK. She asked if I'd be safe and what would my cell be like. Louise generally doesn't show her emotions, she doesn't show her feelings although we are all very close. In a letter to me she told me she loved me. She hugged and kissed me on visits. This is completely abnormal behaviour for her. Louise was also looking for solicitors for me online. She shouldn't have ever had to do that.'* After her mother's return home problems continued: *Louise spends much more time with us. She comes everywhere with us now and seems very insecure. She keeps asking if I could go back to prison and is there any other reasons that might mean I got a sentence. She panics in case bills don't get paid, and needs to know when I've paid them, in case I go back to prison. She has become very clingy.*

The testimony of Sally is equally poignant:

> *My kids are still affected by it. The little one has nightmares. I think my middle one is using cannabis. And my eldest daughter is old beyond her years because she had to look after her sisters when I was away. My middle daughter is still angry with me, but we're getting there.'*

Several of the mothers noted that their children now resent them for having been in prison. Cassy, for example, wrote: '*I think the kids hate me a bit for going to jail.*' For Sandra, as for several of the mothers in our group, imprisonment meant that her children had to be separated, and were placed with different carers. On her return, Sandra stated her baby did not recognise her and didn't want to know her; '*it took ages to bond with her again'*. She goes on to say, the others '*all changed towards each other'* and were '*not so close'* after the separation. Sandra believes that her 16-year-old daughter would not have become pregnant if she, as her mother, had been at home. She wrote:

> *I don't think my kids will ever be the same people they were going to be. As brothers and sisters, they are changed forever for the worse. The one positive is that the kids are closer to their dads, but now they are less close to me, so it's not a positive really.*

The mothers who had to separate their children to go to different carers expressed great concern and upset at this separation of siblings. They were concerned that the children's' feelings towards each other would change, and more than one mother reported that this had in fact occurred.

Michelle's children too were split up (three-year-old daughter and twin boys age 2) and were *'distressed and confused'* as a result. The twins are clingy and needy after the separation. The long-term effect of separating the children has been that her children are *'not as close as they used to be'.* Michelle goes on to say:

> *Ellie used to mother the twins and was a lovely sister – now she gets jealous of them and is naughty for attention and that's been the same since I got out – it's getting better but it's took all this time – I think she got used to be on her own when she was at her dad's and she resented having to share me or her toys. The twins I noticed were more clingy and needy. They were quite independent before I went to jail. I worry about what went on when I was away it tortures me in fact, but I'll never really know that they were properly looked after in that time. They stopped sleeping through the night and were just generally more whiney – it took months for me to get them to sleep through the night again and even then, they would only if they were in the same bed. I think it changed them.'*

Anna's children were separated and the family was evicted. Her middle child, age 4, started wetting the bed, *'It is stopping but he still gets anxious if I leave him. The youngest I think feels different about me. I just don't feel as close to her. The oldest one (10) won't talk about it, but I know she was bullied, because I went to prison.'* *'The oldest one still sees the EWO* [Education Welfare Officer] *now'*. Anna observed, *'It's surprising how in five months only there can be a 'new normal'. The kids were in the end quite happy at their dad's, and the middle one misses living with dad'*. Mandy' described how her 4-year-old son was scared of the dogs at the prison and has remained frightened of dogs. Delia's children were in and out of care. They had a very unsettled time while she was in prison. One of her children is still in care over a year after her time in custody. Another of her children rejects her discipline.

Polly said that on her return her children 'played up', *'they were acting out as though they were punishing me for leaving them'.* Melissa reported that her children were initially a bit clingy but that has improved, *'they are glad it that got me to get rid of my ex and are pleased to get me home.'* *'My eldest daughter has exam revision to make up though, but they are OK'* (this daughter cared for the 2 younger children.)   Jade reported that her eldest began to wet the bed again despite having long been dry before she went to prison.   Jenna too reported her child was wary of the dogs, and that this fear hadn't left her. She stated, *'My daughter is scared of dogs. She is very clingy now but also, I think she is always scared I leave her again. She panics if I'm not on time at school.'*

Long-lasting anxiety and insecurity were features of many of the accounts of the effects on children. Ethel eloquently reported:

> *My middle one started wetting the bed when I went to prison [he was 4 at the time] – it's stopping now – but he still gets anxious if I leave him. The baby, I think, feels different about me – I just don't feel as close to her – but maybe that's my guilt. The oldest one won't talk about it but I know she was bullied because I went to prison. When I came out of prison I thought life would go back to normal. … But I don't think things will ever be the same again. I have a distance with my eldest I can't seem to get over. My son still wets the bed and he was dry before I went to prison. He is an anxious soul now and again. I know it affected him badly and he had nightmares about his dad disappearing too. My eldest was bullied at school [she had to change school when she went to stay with her father]. The school are keeping an eye on Mary to make sure it's all stopped now but I think she is just really embarrassed and ashamed of me actually, which obviously makes me feel beyond guilty. I have so much to make up [to my children]. They shouldn't have suffered because of what I did – I think that's wrong. There were other ways to punish me and that be fair enough, I deserved it, but I don't think they had to be punished too. I just don't think that was fair. I hate myself for what happened really. Can't change it though, can I?*

Betty wrote: *'It damaged me and damaged my kids, the middle ones started wetting the bed and still haven't stopped'.*

There have been long lasting effects on Clare's children. *'My children have been affected by me having to leave them. They had never been without me. I have never committed a crime and therefore to send me to prison was a horrific injustice. It's made myself and my children very vulnerable and scared that I may leave them again'.*

Debbie said that she missed contact visits with her older children, and they didn't understand. *'They played up and I know they were hurt, especially my oldest who said I'd let her down again.* Debbie reported that as a result of feeling shed let her children down, she found it difficult to discipline them, *'as I have so much to make up for'.*

Sandra felt her prison sentence had had a huge impact on her family, her children's father and grandmother cared for them whilst she was in prison. She wrote:

> *The kids miss their dads and their nanas, my middle daughter only comes home at weekends now. I tried making her come but she was miserable, so what can you do. It feels like we are all separate, not like one whole family.*

8. Help and support, agency involvement, the role of PACT

i. Agencies, Grandmothers /Family

The most frequent source of support cited again and again by the participants was from their mothers. Two of the mothers returned to live 'at home' with their mother's post release, with one mother describing how her and her mother now co parent her son, *'now we are almost mum and dad to Robbie, we parent him together, it makes life less stressful for me'.* Post release, Polly was one of several mothers who reported that she *relied* on her mother for support. She stated:

> *Probation was useless – but I didn't feel I needed it anyway. I only needed my mum.*

Mandy was supported by her mum, during her sentence, and post release. She stated '*My mum had my son, and she managed, she is a coper. I think she did find it tough having a youngster at her age, especially full time...but my mum would never have moaned'.* Mandy credits her mother for the fact her son coped well with their separation, stating '*he coped because he was with my mum and she was great, it made us closer I think. Before [prison] we used to argue, although we had a difficult relationship when I got out for a bit, but in the end, we are closer'.*

In two cases sisters were a source of support. Some reported help from the fathers of their children, with significantly higher numbers than expected being temporarily in the role of primary carer during the mother's sentence (29% as opposed to the 9% figure most often quoted); and despite them not being currently in a relationship with the children's mother. Lily was the exception to this, she described a very close and loving relationship with her husband, who suffers from depression and panic attacks and for whom she is the main carer.

Several agencies were cited as helpful. The Community Psychiatric Nurse is mentioned as a source of support for more than one mother, as are friends, the children's school, and a counsellor. Cassy, for example, wrote: '*I had a CPN – the Social [Services] were involved before my kids went to their dads, but not after. … There was a meeting at school. The school were good & had a meeting.* [After release] *I saw my CPN again after a bit – but I had to wait again.*' One mother reported that Social Services had helped her mother while she took on the care of her child, and another that her church was especially helpful and supportive, both during her sentence and post release. One mother found the school helped her child who was bullied – '*they contacted a charity that works with kids with a parent in prison – I was glad about that*'.

Several mothers found post custodial support challenging because of the distance they had to travel to report and the cost of attending appointments. Some mothers mentioned, particularly those who had to take their children with them, that they had to report alongside people with obvious substance misuse and mental health issues.

Several mothers mentioned that they had actively avoided seeking support. For example, Sally didn't tell her children's school that she was in prison because she was '*scared they would tell social services. So, my kids kept it a secret the whole time too.*' (She served 4 months in prison, for a first offence). Others mentioned avoiding social services in particular because, as Mandy put it, '*they take your kids and you don't get them back*'.

ii. Prison Staff and Prison Advice and Care Trust (PACT)

Some of the mothers provided examples of positive care from a variety of prison staff, including a probation officer, prison officers and nursing staff. Jade stated; '*there was one officer who was nice, if it wasn't for her I'd have topped myself*'. Sally reported, '*the nursing staff were angels, really good, and my PO, (probation officer)*'. Melissa also described being able to speak with staff, gaining support, enabling her to feel strong enough to leave an abusive partner. Another mother felt supported by the prison chaplain. Delia who describes herself as having a '*severe*' substance abuse issue, reported she was seen by the prison inreach mental health team, she feels she was treated with '*compassion*'. Mandy, who was pregnant when sentenced reported, '*actually all of the prison staff were good to me*'.

However there appeared little consistency in relation to the mothers' experiences of prison staff. Michelle reported that she felt staff were dismissive of her as a pregnant woman, and stated the *'staff didn't seem bothered'*. One mother stated, *'they treat me like shite and made me feel worse about myself'*. Polly had mixed experiences, stating *'I learned that prison officers don't care... actually that's not true some were lovely, but most were awful'*. However, Polly did state PACT *'were amazing'*.

Indeed, the most consistent positive comments were in relation to PACT staff. The Prison Advice and Care Trust (PACT) (https://www.prisonadvice.org.uk/) is a national charity that provides support to prisoners, people with convictions, and their families. The help of PACT was very much appreciated by many of the participants. Ethel and Jenna reported that PACT was extremely helpful, Ethel said, 'the PACT lady was *amazing'*, *'PACT was wonderful'* reported Jenna. *'My PACT person was really wonderful'*. Jenna reported that PACT arranged for her daughter to visit, Jenna, who was 100 miles from home reported that without the support of PACT arranging a visit she would not have seen her daughter at all during her 17-week sentence.

Mothers appreciated the 'PACT letter'[22], via PACT Mandy was able to send two additional letters a week and had two phone calls. She reports that without PACT *'we wouldn't have seen each other'*. Polly too mentioned the help and support provided by PACT: *'PACT helped me with letters and I think they told mum they would help with visits.'*

Sally said: *'PACT gave me a letter once a week, and once I had to speak to the school and they let me use the office phone.'* Rose reported: *'There was a lovely lady from PACT who came to check my contacts were going OK. Other girls needed her more than me, but she was lovely, very caring'.*

Jenna also credited PACT with helping her through her sentence, *'If it wasn't for the PACT woman, I wouldn't have coped. I think they should do the supervision outside, they are the only ones who helped me'*. Ethel, stated, that although she didn't need the services offered by PACT, *'the PACT lady came to see me to make sure my contacts were all going well. A lovely lady, very caring'.*

---

[22] PACT will supply mothers with one stamped letter home per week. The letter is not on prison paper. In contrast, in Ireland, at the cost of the prison service, mothers are permitted up to seven pre-paid letters per week, in addition they are provided with a 5 minute phone call home (Irish Penal Reform Trust) http://www.iprt.ie/

9. Post Custody

i. Housing and eviction

Four mothers were evicted during their period in prison, with another eviction 'pending'. This is, clearly, a devastating consequence of a short period of imprisonment. Debbie reported:

> I lost my house and had to start again. I found it impossible because I couldn't get a house because I was under 35 and my 18-month-old daughter wasn't living with me. I hoped that someone would help with that but they didn't'. Anna wrote: 'Being evicted means landlords won't give me a chance and the council don' make me a high priority because I don't have my kids yet, but I can't get them because I don't have a home. So, I'm stuck.

Mothers who were not evicted reported coming out of prison to rent arrears and feelings of stress and vulnerability in relation to their housing situation. Two mothers reported their sisters moved into their properties to 'protect the tenancy', causing disruption to their own families and children, which was described as a further source of guilt and stress by the mothers.

ii. Supervision after imprisonment[23]

Many participants, said they would have liked to have had help in relation to housing and other practical issues, after their imprisonment but did not necessarily feel this was available to them. The remark above by Debbie, whose imprisonment led to eviction is typical of this view.

Sally was required to attend supervision 'only once', but as it was in a women's centre and she found it *'really helpful'*, she continued to attend. She said if she had known about the women's centre before she got into trouble she didn't think she would ever have broken the law. *'If I had known about the women's centre before I got into trouble I never would have. They are wonderful to me and my kids. And that's why I go there still after all this time. One day I want to work here.'* Sally, who did experience positive supervision wrote:

> My probation worker has been excellent, she's offered to ring the college for my

---

[23] See Footnote 14

> *daughter and sort it all out, which is great as we are too embarrassed. She's doing stuff to help me get ready for work, I think she will help me get a job which will be amazing. She helped me write a sorry to my victim too*

Several of our participants said that the supervision they received after imprisonment was not in any way helpful. Polly, for example, wrote that *'They told me they could help me budget'* but she found meeting with supervising officers difficult, *'It was too much – there was nothing to say'*; they did not help with housing or other issues *'They couldn't even help me get into work … it was pointless.'*

Jade reported that she was supervised in the community and that she saw about 6 different people and that they offered *'Nothing, it was a check in … It was pointless'*. She objected to the expense to get to the office, and felt there was no help available to her. Jenna was offered counselling and had many meetings with a counsellor. She said what was helpful was *'not probation but counselling'*. Mothers highlighted the cost of attending appointments and one mother, who had a previous breach for missed appointments, stated *'It's alright saying the ticket will be refunded when you get there, but you have to have the money for the ticket in the first place'*.

Significantly, although all the mothers reported some challenges re-integrating with their families, none of the mothers reported any formal support in this area.

iii. Resettlement in the community

All the mothers in the study described some post custodial challenges. For several mothers, this often related to housing and poverty or financial difficulties. Mothers described, issues relating to rent arrears, and issues relating to securing immediate access to any income (either related to work or claiming benefits).

However, by far the most significant challenges the mothers reported, were in relation to re-uniting with their children and re-integrating themselves into the family. All bar one of the mothers, reported negative emotions that troubled them and haunted their relationships with their children. Sally wrote: *'We are delighted to be together again. My middle daughter is still angry with me, but we are getting there. But I don't think I'll ever get over the shock or shame of prison'*.

Ethel struggled with feeling her children were deeply affected by her 21 weeks in prison; She reported:

> *When I came out of prison, I thought life would just go back to normal. Maybe that was naïve I guess, but I did. But I don't think things will ever be the same again. I have a distance with my eldest that I can't seem to get over, the baby is so independent and not at all bothered about being the mummy's' girl she was before I went away. I know that might be good for her in the long run, but it hurts knowing that changed because of me.*

Michelle, despite serving only 9 weeks in custody, reported:

> *It took a long time to readjust to all living together again. Everything changed in those few short weeks. Their dads now have more involvement which I suppose is a good thing, but it took a long time to feel normal again. I still get nightmares about not getting out of prison.*

Lily said that she was seeing a counsellor for help with the trauma of her imprisonment. Clare too who suffered from domestic abuse for a long period, was able after her imprisonment to access support. She wrote '*I have had support from a Connect worker, [name of women's centre] I, the one and only support in eight years.*' Clare found returning home very difficult: '*I suffered PTSD and found it very difficult when I came home. I found I was unable to do even the simplest of things such as post a letter*'. Debbie was clear about what could have helped. '*Sort out problems that cause addiction and give ex-cons a chance. I don't see a bright future but I've learnt to deal with scraping through better*' Anna expressed frustration about having been evicted and being unable to find housing. She wrote: '*I just want to sort out myself and money and homes.*'

10. What helped and what could have helped in our participants' view

Participants in our research felt that custodial sentences are being used inappropriately for women, especially those who have young children, and expressed frustration and concern that prison takes mothers away from their children often for crimes which warrant only very short sentences and pose no risk to the public. Several mothers identified what they would have liked to have experienced in terms of support and supervision. Polly reported, '*I think something to get me back to work would have been good but now I think I won't get a job with a record*'. However, several mothers identified that support or 'help' sooner and in the community, would have been beneficial, with several stating they felt this would have prevented them from going to prison.

Melissa, who was able to access support for domestic abuse in prison stated:

> *'I feel sad that I had to go to prison to get any support for myself and my children. I had asked for help before going to prison and not got it.'*

Jade was very clear that she felt her own post custody supervision was lacking, but identified for her what would have helped;

> *I know I said the separation meant I wouldn't offend again – but I think a community centre (women's centre?) would have looked at my mental health and looked at what makes me impulsive, that would have been better. My friend did that, I looked in her workbook and followed the course she did in it and that was more helpful to me than anything probation or prison did for me.*

Sandra felt that *'prison only makes things worse'*, and that access to community support and understanding for addiction issues would be more beneficial. Ethel reported, *'if I'd had more help, I wouldn't have offended in the first place'*.

Rose, who reported her offence was a 'one off', stated:

> *What those women need, especially the young ones, is help not punishment. I think helping women earlier and better would assist. For women like me, I'm not sure, maybe more understanding of depression and how that can make women act out of character.*

G. Summary and Conclusion

Although the sample in this research was relatively small with 17 participants, the women were mothers to **fifty** children in total. Fifty 'innocent' children affected by the imprisonment of their mother, 43 separated from their mothers as a direct result of their imprisonment. Without exception, the mothers felt their prison sentence had resulted in some negative impact on their children.

This negative impact included children being 'clingy' and 'insecure', bedwetting, nightmares, challenging behaviour, sibling rivalry, sibling separation, bullying and loss of education. The eldest children of three mothers in the study became their younger siblings' carers, two of those leaving full time education to do so. One mother in the study was insistent that her teenage daughter's pregnancy was directly related to her being in prison, and therefore not able to supervise her daughter (the baby was adopted), another felt that her child's cannabis use was also related to her prison sentence for a similar reason. The views of mothers in this study, regarding the impact on their children, and despite their sentences being short or very short; are powerful and should not be ignored. The evidence provided by the mothers supports evidence presented in previous research (Murray and Farrington 2008, Barnardo's 2013), leaving us to conclude that sentence length does not directly correlate to harm caused, again supporting previous research findings (Trebilcock and Dockley 2015). This study supports the view that imprisonment of mothers, even for short periods (weeks as opposed to months), can have a devastating and profound impact on children. As one mother stated simply, *'everything changed in those few short weeks'* (Michelle).

The report highlights again the significant impact of short custodial sentences on mothers and their children. The pain in the responses of the mothers was evident, 'guilt', 'shame', and 'worry' were mentioned by most. There is no doubt that for the mothers in this study the root source of these emotions, was in relation to the separation from their children. Particularly striking in this research, was the impact on the older children, in terms of complex emotional dynamics between mother and child; but also, impact in relation to the older children; becoming carers. This means having to interrupt or give up on 'childhood' education, and take on 'adult' responsibilities prematurely. Although none of the mothers in this study were mothers of adult offspring, as Baldwin (forthcoming, 2017) and Wahidin (2004) have noted, mothers of adult offspring often experience the same anxiety and trauma by being separated from their 'children' and grandchildren, as mothers of younger children; Petra Puddepha, from Wahidin's study, stated simply, '*You never stop being a mother, you're a mother till the day you die'* (2004:176). Baldwin (ibid) identifies that mothers of adults, often feel *'layers'* of emotion and pain because of their imprisonment, particularly fearing the judgement and loss of children **and** grandchildren, as well as the pain of separation. This is an area often overlooked in research.

Visits, which one might assume would feel positive from the mother's perspective, were often actually a source of additional stress and heartache. Mothers worried about the cost, and time away from school it often meant for children. Some of the mothers found the visits restrictive, emotional and challenging. Thought needs to be given to facilitate, consistently, more child friendly, appropriate visiting spaces, with consideration given to the way in which children are affected by security measures (i.e. dogs, restrictions on physical contact).

Significantly, the challenges and issues for mothers and their children did not end with the period of imprisonment. Mothers felt practical, problem solving support was lacking from the post release supervision. Some mothers felt that lack of 'useful' support on release left them vulnerable to re-offending. As one mother put it, *'I don't need to talk about what I did wrong, I need actual help so I don't do it again'.*

As highlighted by this report, mothers experienced significant challenges in relation to re-integration into their families, particularly into their mothering role. The responses of the mothers were heavy with not only the pain of separation and the challenges they faced being an imprisoned mother, but also, they gave testimony to the fact that their worries as mothers did not end with the sentences. Many mothers spoke of how they would continue to feel guilt and shame about their sentence, and would continue to worry and wonder how their sentence had affected their children, and would so for years to come.

There is no doubt that some of the women described a number of 'positives' that had come about because of their prison sentence (although outweighed for all, by the negatives). These positives are a learning opportunity, to lay and inform foundations for consistent work across the sector in relation to 'what works with women', and how best the women themselves feel they need to be supported in order to maximise rehabilitation and desistance.

One of our main conclusions is regarding sentencing. Sentencing is the 'gateway' to reducing the women's prison population significantly and swiftly. Epstein (2012), Baldwin (2015), and Minson (2014), have all previously identified sentencing as a point offering a significant opportunity for change in relation to mothers, calling for routine consideration to be given as to the needs and rights of the child at the point of sentencing. All have offered proposals for positive change. Their proposals were echoed by the Prison Reform Trust (PRT) in its Discussion Paper, 'Sentencing of Mothers: Improving the Sentencing Process and Outcomes for Women with Dependent Children' (2015).[24] The PRT paper recommendations remain valid.

All the mothers whose voices can be heard in this paper, were sentenced to short terms for minor and nonviolent offences. Yet the suffering caused, to them and to

---

[24] See also Footnote 3

their dependent children was great, arguably in most circumstances, no less, and sometimes more, than those who are sentenced to 12 months or more. The mothers and children faced the same challenges in terms of lack of support, complex needs, difficulties regarding visits and contact, loss of housing and impact on physical and mental health. Similarly, the children, as described by their mothers, were traumatised simply by the separation, regardless of the length of their mother's imprisonment.

On 4 November 2015, the then Minister of Justice Michael Gove said at the AGM of the Howard League for Penal Reform that he believed our sentencing framework needed a complete overhaul. He recognised that evidence shows short sentences are more likely than not to lead to recidivism, and that the system needs a more appropriate sentencing framework[25].

As previously stated, the law requires that prison be used as a sanction only when the offence is 'so serious' that it cannot be punished by a fine or a community sentence. Most women in prison have not committed violent offences (over 80%). The most recent Ministry of Justice prison reception data reveals that theft and handling offences account for 41% of all custodial sentences given to women. The argument is sometimes raised that prison is necessary for repeat offenders, but 28% of all sentenced women are in prison for a first offence, compared to 12% of men (PRT 2015). Furthermore, the number of women recalled to prison for breach has escalated rapidly. The Prison Reform Trusts' recent response to the to the Sentencing Council consultation on breach guidelines (2017)[26], identified that there had been an, 81% increase in women being recalled to prison between 2015 and 2016. Further stating that 'on 30th June 2016, women recalled to custody accounted for nearly 8% of the total prison population' (PRT, 2017,2).

There is evidence that, where the terms of a non-custodial sentence disregard a woman's responsibility for children, there is an increased risk of breach for non-compliance (Jordon 2013). Breaches can in turn lead to custodial sentences

---

[25] Gove admits the UK sentencing framework needs to be more sensitive, & 7 more things we learned at the 2015 Howard League AGM", Halsbury's Law Exchange.

[26] See: Prison Reform Trust response to the to the Sentencing Council consultation on breach guidelines (2017) http://www.prisonreformtrust.org.uk/Portals/0/Documents/Consultation%20responses/Sentencing%20Council%20consultation%20on%20breach.pdf

being imposed where imprisonment was outside the sentencing parameters for the original offence. It is important therefore that community sanctions are mindful of women's childcare responsibilities and priorities, and that the 'breach regime is flexible and not overly punitive (PRT 2017).[27]

Many mothers described the cost of attending appointments as challenging, Current practice sees most supervisees having to pay out for transport costs to appointments and claim back retrospectively. Thought and respect needs to be given for just how financially restricted some families are, with consideration given to a means of pre-payment for transport costs, (e.g. a permit for travel on public transport).

Furthermore, guidance provided by the 'Bangkok Rules', adopted by the UN General Assembly (Resolution A/RES/65/229)[28] must be universally applied. Had the sentencing guidelines and rules been consistently applied, many of the women in this study may not have been imprisoned, and fifty children would not have been negatively affected by their mother's incarceration.

Alongside the need for positive change in relation to sentencing, this research has highlighted the need for positive change in relation to pre-custodial and post custodial support for mothers and their children. In addition, the report draws attention to the need for those providing temporary childcare for imprisoned mothers to be more formally and appropriately supported.

H. Recommendations

On the basis of our findings we strongly endorse and reiterate the Prison Reform Trust conclusions and recommendations. The PRT discussion paper recommends:

1. The government should review the sentencing framework to ensure appropriate recognition of and provision for an offender's sole or primary care responsibilities, in relation to both custodial and non-custodial sentencing.

---

[27] See Sue Jordan's research on women who breached community orders (Jordan, S. (2013) "Missing voices: Why women engage with, or withdraw from, community sentences", Research Paper 2013/01 London: The Griffins Society).

[28] United Nations Rules for The Treatment of Female Prisoners and Non-Custodial Measures for Women Offenders (known as the Bangkok Rules). https://www.penalreform.org/resource/united-nations-bangkok-rules-women-offenders-prisoners-short/

2. The government's Advisory Board on Female Offenders should review arrangements in the criminal justice system for women with primary or sole care responsibilities considering s10 of the Offender Rehabilitation Act 2014, and ensure a whole of government approach to improving outcomes for mothers and their children, including coordinated and consistent funding streams for women's services and interventions.

3. Sentencing guidelines should be strengthened by the addition of an "overarching principle" setting out the court's duty to investigate sole or primary caring responsibilities of defendants and to take these responsibilities into account in sentencing. This would reflect the Court of Appeal decision in *R v Petherick*.

4. Courts should establish mechanisms to ensure the provision of sufficient information to sentencers where the offender has primary caring responsibilities, including a requirement for a full written pre-sentence report and a local directory of women's services and interventions.

5. When imposing non-custodial sentences, sentencers must inquire about and consider a woman's family responsibilities and ensure 'rehabilitation activity requirements' are achievable within those constraints.

6. Judges, district judges and magistrates should be obliged to consider non-custodial sentences for offenders with primary care responsibilities, and in cases when imprisonment is an option should consider a community order, deferred or suspended sentence. If an immediate term of imprisonment is imposed, written reasons should be given for their decision.

7. Training bodies, including the Judicial College, the Law Society and the Bar Council, should ensure sufficient emphasis in both induction training and continuing education on the balancing exercise to be undertaken when sentencing an offender with sole or primary care responsibilities.

We reiterate the need for a reformed sentencing policy, one which reflects the strength of feeling and breadth of research in relation to the harms of custodial sentences for women, particularly mothers; most importantly one that reflects the voices and experiences of women who tell us time and time again that prison, at best doesn't work, at worst causes long term harm to them and their children. These proposals should be implemented without delay. We further recommend:

1. We suggest that alongside gender specific training in relation to the judiciary and criminal justice professionals, it would be right to develop **gender specific sentencing guidelines.** Player (2005) identified that '*Treating offenders equally has often been interpreted as treating them uniformly, resulting in particular*

problems for the fair treatment of women because it is based on a presumptive male subject'. Gender specific sentence guidelines would be much more likely to ensure that women were sentenced appropriately and in consideration of their and their children's best interests. Developing and implementing gender specific guidelines would potentially have a faster impact than the complete overhaul of the sentencing framework argued for above (and would perhaps meet with less resistance).

2. Community based non-custodial options must be the 'go to' sentence in all but the most serious of offences for women. We recommend following Scotland's lead in relation to a presumption against short sentences, ideally of less than 12 months (which Scotland are considering, after the success of the presumption against 3-month sentences)[29]. We further suggest abandoning any plans to build more women's prisons and diverting funds to support community initiatives (as recommended by Liz Hogarth in her recent report),[30]Furthermore, appropriate and permanent funding should be allocated to ensure that women's services remain available in the community, with the intention to divert women away from the CJS.

3. We would also wish to see a presumption against pregnant mothers being sentenced to custody, in all but the most extreme of circumstances. That's not to say we don't feel that MBU's play a valuable role in supporting vulnerable mothers and their babies, in contact with the CJS, (particularly mothers with addiction issues), we do, but we see no reason for such places to be located within a prison. Successful mother/child therapeutic communities exist, see for example Trevi House, and Coolmine, Ireland, both work with mothers who have substance misuse issues and are therefore vulnerable to becoming entrenched in the CJS)[31]. Such models could be extended. We propose that 'Birth

---

[29] https://www.crimeandjustice.org.uk/resources/action-needed-short-prison-sentences-scotland

[30] Hogarth, L. (2017) Trapped in the Justice Loop? Past, present and future of the woman-centred services at the heart of the systems-change called for in the Corston Report. Centre for Crime and Justice Studies. https://www.crimeandjustice.org.uk/sites/crimeandjustice.org.uk/files/Trapped%20in%20the%20Justice%20Loop%2C%20May%202017.pdf

[31] Trevi House, Plymouth. residential rehabilitation programme for women together with their children, with drug and alcohol dependency issues http://www.treviproject.org/ See also; Coolmine Ashleigh House: Women & children residential Ashleigh House is a residential Therapeutic Community for women, expectant women and mothers with young children. Ashleigh House is designed to help women in recovery develop the skills they need to live a drug-free, independent life. By providing a supportive setting our clients can build on their self-confidence, emotional management and the relapse prevention skills needed to remain addiction free. http://www.coolmine.ie/services-new/residentials/

Companions'[32], would be ideal partners to act as consultants, with a view to developing nationwide community based resources for mothers affected by, or at risk of being affected by, the criminal justice system. They would be ideally placed to advise on their development, incorporating principles similar to those outlined in their 'Birth Charter'[33].

4. We recommend that systematic recording of the *actual* number of mothers in custody, the numbers of children affected, and their whereabouts whilst mothers are in prison, be actioned without delay. However, it is important that this information is gathered in a non-threatening way and via non-threatening means.

5. Importantly, consideration needs to be given to facilitate the permanent funding of organizations such as PACT, who clearly play a significant role in the lives of women who do end up in prison. Prisons having devolved budgets may be the ideal opportunity for such organizations to be permanently 'factored in'. One mother, so appreciative of the service she had had in custody, suggested PACT '*should take over community supervision*'.

6. We would urge a return with vigour, to the recommendations of the Corston report, with renewed investment into women's center support. We wholeheartedly agree with the recommendations of the 'Women in Prison' Corston+10 report, which argues that women '*not only do women need to be diverted away from custody, but also need diverting toward support in the community*'. It is therefore vital that wise investment ensures that such support is indeed available.

7. We would like to see more formal recognition and support for those caring for children of imprisoned parents, and the children themselves, emotionally and practically. We would also suggest prison establishments explore ways in which they can actively support and assist in maintaining family relationships and positive family contact, particularly when mothers face additional challenges such as distance or children who have been split up across more than one location.

---

[32] See also 16.

[33] The Birth Charter is a set of recommendations for the care of pregnant women and new mothers in prison developed in consultation with our service users and with guidance from the Royal College of Midwives and UNICEF UK Baby Friendly Initiative. The Birth Charter has been developed to help inform the Government's review of the treatment of these vulnerable women and their babies, and to improve current practice across the Prison Service. http://www.birthcompanions.org.uk/Birth-Charter

8. We recommend in cases where custody of a primary carer with dependent children is inevitable, that there is a short delay, of a period up to 7 days, before the custodial sentence begins. This would facilitate the arrangement of childcare responsibility and allow time for the dependent children to emotional and physically prepare for separation.

9. Given the number of mothers who expressed difficulty in maintaining contact, both physically and via telephone, we suggest there is an urgent need to explore ways in which communication for mothers and children can be improved, supported and maintained. Perhaps we can learn from Ireland where the prison service absorbs the cost of both phone calls and letters home, enabling women to speak to their children, sometimes daily[34], with at least one letter weekly (O'Malley and Devaney 2015).

10. This research echoes the early findings of Baldwin's parallel doctoral research, exploring the emotional impact of imprisonment on mothers; in that mothers in custody need to be supported in their role as mothers[35], pre-custody, during their sentence and importantly, post release; *'If we are to continue to imprison mothers, then the penal systems need to respect and account for their maternal needs and responsibilities, and to explore ways in which maternal identity and relationships can be enhanced.'* (Baldwin, 2017;7).

I. Suggested further research

Recommendations for further research include continued analytical focus on how mothers affected by the criminal justice system can be better supported during their sentence and post release. Importantly, also how mothers can be better supported to ensure they do not enter custody in the first instance. To do this, comprehensive research needs to be undertaken to ascertain accurate characteristics and statistics surrounding mothers who encounter the CJS, and those in prison, i.e. the *actual* number of mothers in prison, along with accurate

[34] O'Malley and Devaney (2015;27). 'Along with direct contact visits there are additional contact opportunities for mothers and their children within the prison. In the main this takes the form of telephone contact or letters. According to participants, all adult prisoners are permitted at least one telephone call per week with women prisoners permitted one six-minute telephone call every day. Telephone calls can be made to a maximum of six telephone numbers, one of which must be their solicitor. In addition, a newly implemented "Incentivised Regime" allows that, following a period of six to eight weeks in prison, women can be awarded an extra daily six-minute telephone call. Participants explained how this additional call is vital for maintaining mother–child contact particularly in situations where mothers have more than one child who may be looked after by a number of different carers:

[35] Baldwin, L. Mothers in prison; 'Tainted love'; The Impact of Prison on Mothering Identity Explored via Mothers' Post Prison Reflections. *Prison Service Journal* (Forthcoming, 2017).

statistics in relation to the number who were primary carers at the point of sentence, who will be post release, and what happens to their children.

It is important to establish, since the implementation of TR and statutory post release supervision, how women have been affected in practice. Trebilcock and Dockley (2015) highlighted the risk of women being *'up tariffed'*, in an effort to access support, and /or being returned to court (and possibly prison) for 'failing to comply' with supervision requirements. The extension of statutory supervision to short sentences has effectively increased the prisoner population. Recalls of short sentenced prisoners has increased dramatically. For women, the number recalled to custody whilst under supervision, has increased by over four fifths, (82%) since the end of 2014. Therefore, post TR research to explore the impact of the criminal justice reforms on women and their families is thus imperative, and we would argue, urgent.

It is suggested that further research is needed in relation to the subsequent relationship dynamics (both positive and negative), between mothers affected by the criminal justice system, their families and their children; in order that they are more appropriately and effectively supported. We feel this is particularly important in relation to, what we feel is the under researched area, of mothers of older and adult offspring.

Most of the mothers in this study reported being supported by their own mothers, often prior to, during, and after their release from prison. Paternal grandmothers also played a supporting role. Grandmothers were the main carers for 7 of the mothers in this study (41%). Baldwin recently completed a small-scale study[36] exploring relationships and the impact on grandmothers when a daughter is imprisoned (also exploring Grandmothering from prison). This research will assist in understanding the impact on grandmothers as carers of children with a parent in prison, however further research on a broader scale would contribute, not only to the recognition of these 'unsung heroines' (Raikes 2016), but would assist in ascertaining the needs of this group and therefore how best they can be, and should be, supported.

It is clear from the participants' reports, that the delays they experienced in receiving their medication, had a direct and negative impact on their mental

---

[36] Baldwin L. (2017), 'Grandmothering in the Context of Criminal Justice: Grandmothers in Prison and Grandmothers as Carers when a Parent is Imprisoned'. (Forthcoming)

health. Given the fact that suicide and self-harm rates are currently at their highest ever level, it would seem pertinent to explore, via further research, the relationship, if there is any, between delays in medication and subsequent suicide and self-harm incidents.

We would suggest that future research be undertaken surrounding the 'positives', as described by a few participants. A small number of mothers in the study described 'positives' which came about because of their sentence, further research is needed to establish whether such positives are *only* the result of mothers simply 'making the best of a bad job', (as one mother described), or perhaps relate to being able to access resources that had not been easily accessible in the community (as was described by another); or, if indeed something can be learned in relation to using the positives mothers described more consistently and effectively, with a view to informing change both inside and outside custody.

Lastly, given the small-scale nature of this study, repeating the study on a larger scale may offer a richer source of information, from which clear recommendations may evolve.

Highlighting the findings of this study and the further research suggested above, to those responsible for judicial and penal policy and practice, may result, we would hope, in more positive outcomes for mothers and their children.

J. Appendix

Contents

i. Table 1. Data on offence, sentence, ethnicity, ages and circumstances of children.

ii. Table 2. Data showing care arrangements, visits, healthcare and support in prison

iii. Table 3. Data on impact on health, housing, level of support and effects of sentence on children

iv. Council tax debt

Why it is normally unlawful to sentence someone to imprisonment for council tax debt

i. Tables.

Table 1: Data on offence, sentence, ethnicity, ages and circumstances of children.

No.	Pseudonym	Offence	Time served	Ethnicity	Ages of children	Pre-existing vulnerabilities	Vulnerabilities of children
1	Clare	Council Tax debt (1st offence)	7 weeks	White British	7, 17	Domestic abuse	Non-specified
2	Lily	Council Tax debt (1st offence)	2 weeks	White British	16	Primary carer for partner. Also has depression, epilepsy, anxiety.	Suffers anxiety/can't attend school
3	Anna	Benefit fraud, shoplifting	13 weeks	White Irish	4 children	Depression, alcohol dependency, self-harm, substance misuse (historical), debt problems.	1 in care at point of sentence
4	Betty	Fraud/non-payment of fines	9 weeks	White Irish	4, 6, 7, 17	Alcohol dependency	Youngest child disabled One daughter self-harms
5	Cassy	GBH	13 weeks	White English	9, 11	Depression, earlier suicide attempt, has a CPN*, self-harm, panic attacks (started in prison)	Mother lost custody after offence
6	Debbie	Shoplifting baby formula, nappies; previous suspended sentence)	34 weeks	White English	18 months, 4, 9, 11	Addiction problems, anxiety, post-partum depression, debt problems	3 children in care, have FAS, baby living at home
7	Delia	Non-violent off (drugs related)	6weeks -12 months (several sentences)	Not stated	19,16,8, 3 (younger when sentenced)	Entered prison with 'crack induced psychosis', and 8 months pregnant, debt problems, substance misuse	Children 'in and out of care'. Mother absconded form court to arrange childcare then later handed herself in.
8	Ethel	Criminal damage, theft	21 weeks	Black British	2, 4, 10	Anxiety, depression	Non-stated

9	Jade	Theft, public order	9 weeks	White Irish	3, 4, 7	History of depression/self harm-Has had help from CPN	Non-stated
10	Jenna	Shoplifting	17 weeks	Welsh	6	Depression, anxiety, Daughter previously in care, then with mum at point of sentence	Child spent time in care after birth, social services involved
11	Mandy	Handling Stolen Goods	9 weeks	White British	4	Pregnant at sentence, anxiety, debt issues.	Non-stated
12	Melissa	Not stated	9 weeks	Black British	5, 11, 17	Depression, diabetes; domestic abuse, assault by partner	Eldest is dyslexic
13	Michelle	Benefit fraud.	9 weeks	White British	2, 2, 3	Depression, on medication, partner with alcohol and anger issues, pregnant at point of sentence.	Twins were premature, health issues
14	Polly	Theft from electric meter	14 weeks	White British	4, 7, 9	Pregnant at sentencing. Debt issues 'caused by benefit sanctions'.	Previous social service involvement with oldest child- not current
15	Sandra	Shoplifting, possession*	13 weeks	Mixed race. British	3, 5, 7, 11, 16 (5 yr. old was 3 months on last sentence)	Pregnant at sentence. Depression and anxiety. History of self-harm and liver disease. Cannabis use.	Eldest has FAS, children separated during sentence.
16	Sally	Fraud (1st offence)	16	White British	17,14,12, 4	Depression, Widowed, Debt issues	14 yr old has 'behavioural issues'. Child already lost father.
17	Rose	Theft from Employer (1st Offence)	26 ½ weeks	Black British	17,12,10	Depression, early menopause related health issues.	Non stated.

Table 2: Data showing care arrangements, visits, healthcare and support in prison

No.	Pseudonym	Who cared for children	Visits and contact	Problems with visits	Experience of visit	Health care in prison	Support during sentence
1	Clare	Children's Father	Elder, yes Younger, no	Only saw one child ex wouldn't bring other child	Upsetting, heart-breaking.	'Negative impact on my health, no help, now have PTSD'	Non-stated
2	Lily	Children's Father	Yes	Costly	Very difficult, 'traumatic' saying goodbye	Not given any medication. for 5 days	Husband
3	Anna	Grandmother & sister	One visit	Distance/expense	'Too painful'	Declined offers of support in prison – 'not in right headspace'	Supported by family (mother/ sister)-
4	Betty	Grandmother	once	'Too dear'	'Not fair on kids'	Nothing specified	Supported by mother
5	Cassy	Father (had custody)	Every 4 weeks	No issues – 'local'	No issues	'It took ages to get my tablets'- refused sleeping pills	From CPN/ friends
6	Debbie	Grandmother (3 in care)	none	Mother 'refused' to visit prison.130 miles	'Too embarrassed to have them to come'	'Couldn't get regular medications so everything was just worse'.	Social Services helped her mother with the child, which helped her 'by default'.
7	Delia	Sister, then fostered when sister 'couldn't cope'	Yes, after 5 months (longest sentence) not at all on shorter ones	'and stressful Too far, too costly, too difficult to arrange '	'Awful', stressful.	Received 'good' mental health care, support from drug inreach team.	Nothing specified.
8	Ethel	Children's Father	twice	Children were 'embarrassed to come'	Boring for them, older 2 hated visits- felt like hospital visits	No help for her anxiety- felt superficial support	Felt did not get 'useful' support – apart form SAFFA (contacted by PO)
9	Jade	Grandmother had 2, Child father already	once	Mother refused to visit with	'It was awful'	'it's easier to get drugs' – hard to	Mum – stated all support needed was

		had eldest		child more		resist them too'.	from mum.
10	Jenna	Sister	One visit	Home was Wales – prison over 100 miles away. 'Without PACT, we wouldn't have seen each other'	'Stressful-.travel sick – too sick for her to enjoy the visit and she was frightened of the dogs.	'I was stressed all the time – PACT helped, officers weren't so good'.	PACT was wonderful- if it wasn't for the PACT woman I wouldn't have coped
11	Mandy	Grandmother	Weekly	Told son this was 'mummy's work'-	Frightened of the dogs. Painful at the end – especially for grandmother	Pregnant, stated staff were 'good', 'saw a nurse straightaway' found 'all prison staff supportive'.	From mother, now lives with her 'only need mum'. Mum is amazing, a coper'.
12	Melissa	Eldest, aged 17 became full time carer.	Yes, once	Didn't want to 'chew' them to bring them again	It was OK- the children saw it as an adventure. Painful saying goodbye.	Saw a doctor straightaway, diabetic medication 'sorted straightaway'.	Pact were 'good', saw someone who helped me leave behind domestic abuse- saw I dint have to put up with it'.
13	Michelle	Children split, twins at home with father, girl to her dad	Twins once only	Too stressful, how do you explain to 2-year old's they can't be on your knee'	'They were crying and confused, screamed when they left, awful'	Delay in medication 'made me feel suicidal'. Lost her baby 2 weeks into sentence – 'lost it in my cell on my own 'Didn't feel staff were 'bothered' and did not feel 'looked after'.	Felt supported by fellow prisoners only.
14	Polly	Grandmother.	Yes, regular.	Costly. 'The kids were just glad to see me'.	Visits were 'painful'. One was cancelled – that was 'traumatic'.	Pregnant, yet left on her own when spotting. Asked to see midwife. Lost the baby.	Supported by 'the other mums'
15	Sandra	Children split, 2 youngest to dad	No visits	'journey too long and too expensive, so I had no visits'	'Broke my heart not to see them'	It took 'ages' to get tablets sorted, 'so self-harm was at its worst, my depression too'	Nothing stated

| 16 | Sally | Eldest daughter (17) | One visit | 'too far and too expensive' | 'heart-breaking – we all cried from beginning to end' | 'Nearly a week to sort medication' 'at a time when being away from my kids made the lowest id ever felt' 'felt suicidal' | Nursing staff were angels Probation worker 'excellent', Friends supported my daughter |
| 17 | Rose | Eldest daughter (17) | Visits every other week | Costly and children had to miss school to come as driver couldn't come weekends | 'Felt ashamed and embarrassed during them'– kids got to enjoy them 'hard to try to give them all attention' | Felt her 'lady problems 'would have been easier to manage at home 'no understanding at all of my change issues' .Dr refused her HRT. Feels depression got worse and had to wait for medication (10 days) | Own local church very supportive in and after prison PACT very supportive Children's school 'brilliant'. |

Table 3: Data on impact on health, housing, level of support and effects of sentence on children

No.	Pseudonym	Impact on health and well-being	Housing	Support	Effects on children	Stated positives/negatives
1	Clare	PTSD unable to do anything	No issues stated	'Connect' worker in women's centre	Children feel scared all the time I will leave them	'NO positives, all negatives'
2	Lily	Flashbacks, insecure, tearful	No issues stated	Counsellor	Child much more insecure, spends all her time with parents, fearful Mum will go back	As a family, we have all been deeply affected' 'it was torture' No positives.
3	Anna	Anxiety /depression post release	Evicted	Non-specified	1 Child taken into care 2 others live with grandmother and sister	Negatives – contact with separated children difficult, now struggling to gain housing and reunite with children – no positives specified
4	Betty	Feels 'damaged'	No issues stated	Mother	Damaged children, middle ones started bedwetting, this continues	Was 'pleased' she wasn't subject to supervision (pre-TR)
5	Cassy	Has panic attacks/MH issues	Stays with friends	Friends & CPN	Relationship with children worsened- feels 'distant'.	'Quite liked prison, I had good mates' 'Kids hate me for going to prison'.
6	Debbie	Made health issues worse	'lost my house'	Mother & social services	Children angry she missed contact visits, they played up, children felt let down	
7	Delia	Psychosis, was treated well	Evicted on two occasions	Women's Centre MDT	Children in and out of care, one child now in CJS,	Positive effect, good health care- helped with addiction – but disrupted children's lives (although states 'as did addiction')
8	Ethel	Still suffers depression- 'worsened by prison'	Evicted	Mother SAFFA (ex armed forces charity)	Child,4, started bed wetting, it's stopping, he still gets anxious if she leaves. He misses Dad. Eldest child bullied. Middle child has nightmares. Toddler – feels bond is	Ate regular meals, enjoyed security & routine- prison sentenced created debt issues 'damaged the family

				broken.	forever'
9	Jade	Waited 3 1/2 weeks for medication- mental health suffered – still 're balancing'	Eviction pending	'thought would get housing support, but didn't' Supervision 'just a ticky box'. Mum supports her	7-year-old started bed wetting,	Asked about positives replied, 'nothing nothing nothing'. 'losing home because of it, created debt and arrears'. Moving in with Mother (positive)
10	Jenna	'my depression and panic attacks got worse. Prison nearly tipped me over the edge, I did think about suicide.'	Sister moved into house to protect tenancy	'no support, only interference'.	Lives with sister – sister has legal responsibility for daughter. Child is now very clingy, panics if mum/sister is not at school to meet her. 'She's always scared ill leave her'.	Offred counselling post release Prison was not best for me or my daughter. PACT were amazing , I met lovely people.
11	Mandy	'I don't think pregnant women should go to prison – the stress in pregnancy isn't safe'	Now lives with mum	Mother	Child now afraid of dogs,	Now closer to her mother- now living with her but states 'there was nothing positive -nothing at all' (but did state staff were good)
12	Melissa	No issues stated	No issues stated	Counselling arranged by PO- very helpful. Probation 'less so'.	Eldest daughter had to interrupt FT education to care for siblings. Younger children a bit clingy now. Stated 'my children will be forever damaged'.	Was able to access support and guidance that enabled her to leave long standing abusive partner – but feels sad had to go to prison to get it- had asked for help before.
13	Michelle	Miscarried in prison- suffered withdrawals from medication because of delay- felt suicidal – feels traumatized by the experience.	Non-stated – but 'it took a long time to re adjust to living together '	No support – 'I don't know what I needed, but I needed something'.	Children not as close (children were separated), 4 yr old doesn't want to share toys & attention. Children clingy and jealous of each other. The children stopped sleeping through.	Children are now closer to their dads – but at the expense of being close to me '.

14	Polly	Feels deeply affected from losing baby – baby in ambulance, in handcuffs on way to hospital – after being alone spotting in cell	No issues stated	Grandmother- 'Probation was useless but I didn't feel I needed it anyway '. Felt supervision was 'pointless'	Youngest is clingy, middle one got bullied. They now 'act out' – feels like they want to punish me – they are angry'.	'There was nothing to be gained from that sentence, it achieved nothing but getting my child bullied'. 'PACT was amazing'.
15	Sandra	Felt the delay in medication made her 'worse' than she'd ever felt- although is 'clean and sober' now.	Sister temporarily took over her tenancy	Nothing stated	Youngest didn't know her, took ages to bond again, all children unsettled after being away from home with dads/grandparents. 16 yr old got pregnant, child will be adopted. Because they were separated children not as close to each other, one child chose to remain with father.	'All prison did was make me feel like a terrible person'- yes I got sober – but it shouldn't have been prison' 'I made some good friends.'
16	Sally	Depression- feels made worse by prison -delay in medication made her feel suicidal – felt nursing staff were good	Home stable (eldest daughter caring for younger siblings)	Daughter and friend Probation 'excellent' Attended women's Centre – 'kept going voluntarily'.	Eldest child became carer, had to take time out from college – still hadn't returned- middle child 'angry' youngest child 'clingy' – youngest still has nightmares – thinks middle child uses cannabis.	Felt in comparison to others her 'trauma' was less than others- because her 'life history' wasn't 'as bad'- now wishes to work with ex-offenders. 'Prison changes you, not in a good way'
17	Rose	Depression (onset after offence) early menopause – prison Doctor would not prescribe HRT- waited 10 days for medication for depression- feels made her worse	Home stable (eldest daughter carer)	Church Eldest child PACT supported	Eldest child was carer – mum feels sad about this but eldest daughter gained in confidence as a result- not sure if she will return to FT education however.	The positives she stated are 'it has brought us closer as a family ' became a prison listener' and wanted to help other women – but feels it shouldn't have been prison – ' suspended sentence would have been more appropriate , helping women earlier and better would assist'

ii.

Why it is normally unlawful to sentence someone to imprisonment for council tax debt

The law

Under Regulation 47 of the Local Government Finance Act 1992 and the Schedule 2 and Schedule 4 of Local Government Finance Act 1992 and the Council Tax (Administration and Enforcement) Regulations 1992 (SI.1992/613) local authorities may apply to the magistrates' court for a warrant committing a debtor to prison for up to three months. However, the court must make inquiries as to the debtor's means and may only commit to prison if it is satisfied that failure to pay is due to 'wilful refusal or culpable neglect'.

The Act provides that if council tax is not paid as required a magistrates' court may make a liability order against a debtor, which can be enforced by deductions from income support (a jobseeker's allowance or pension state credit).

There is also provision for a magistrates' court to remit the amount outstanding rather than issue a warrant, or to fix a term of imprisonment in default of payment.

Case law

In the 1990's thousands of people who failed to pay the poll tax were sent to prison for periods of up the 3 months. Very few of them challenged their imprisonment. The process of judicial review is not well understood by the public and many legal advisers have had no experience of it.

A few cases did come before the High Court where the decisions by magistrates to commit to prison were challenged. (See Ian Wise and Rona Epstein, Magistrates in the Dock, *New Law Journal*, 21 April 1995). In most of these challenges the magistrates' decisions were declared unlawful and were quashed. The authorities on poll tax imprisonment apply equally to imprisonment for council tax as the statutory provisions are essentially the same.

First, there is no power to send the debtor to prison as a punishment. The powers of the magistrates are coercive not punitive, intended to be exercised only when the debtor has the means to clear the debt. Thus, the sole purpose of issuing a warrant of commitment is to compel the debtor to pay where he has the means to do so. In *R v Leicester Justices ex parte Deary* Brooke J said: '*The court has now repeatedly made clear that the purpose of the powers of the court under Regulation 41 are not the powers of punishment for past misdeeds, but powers to ensure future payment of past liabilities*'.

Neither can the court impose imprisonment as a deterrent to other tax defaulters. In *R v Leeds Magistrates ex parte Meikleham*, Dyson J stated: '*It is clearly established that the purpose of imprisonment is to extract payment by coercion and not to punish ... In my judgment, there is no power in the magistrates to pass a sentence of imprisonment pursuant to Regulation 41(3) as a deterrent. They would not even have been able to pass a deterrent sentence had this been a criminal case. That is the effect of the Criminal Justice Act 1991. In my judgment, it is a fortiori in a case concerned with civil obligations.*'

Debtors must not be imprisoned if there is an alternative: 'It is established that it is wrong in law to pass a sentence of imprisonment when an alternative to imprisonment is available'.

Deduction from state benefit must be considered as an alternative to imprisonment: 'I am quite satisfied that they [the justices] failed to have regard to the purpose of the legislation by failing to consider the alternative of deducting the applicant's arrears from his income support. The failure to consider that alternative was, in my view, an unlawful fetter of their discretion.' And deductions from benefit should be ordered even if the debtor refuses to cooperate. In *R v Hull Justices ex parte Johnson* Schiemann J stated: *'That procedure [to order deductions from social security payments] does not require the co-operation of the debtor apart from an ability of the authority to be able to specify the name and address of the debtor, the name and place of the court which made the liability order, the date when the liability order was made, the total amount of the arrears specified in the liability order and the total amount which the authority wishes to be deducted from income support'.*

The court also has the power to remit the debt. In *R v North and East Hertfordshire Magistrates' Court ex p Dawn Jones* Potts J held that in tax default cases there was an appropriate comparison with fines cases, and in particular *R v Ealing Justices ex p Cloves* (CO/1610/89) where the court said: *'If the defendant cannot pay the fine within a reasonable time, it is an indication that the fine is too high.' Potts J held that a decision requiring a defaulter to pay off her outstanding community charge over a period of 10 years at £1 per week showed that the sum ordered to be repaid was, in the circumstances, too high. The justices should have considered how long it would be right and equitable to require the debtor to repay the arrears and they had failed to do so. Payment under liability orders had to have effect over a reasonable period; otherwise the arrears should be remitted.'*

The *Aldous* case

On 14th January 2011, the Dartford magistrates committed Amanda Aldous to prison for 90 days for failure to pay council tax arrears amounting to approximately £7,000 for the period 2003 to 2009. She is the mother of five children and had been the victim of domestic violence. Her youngest child was aged 15 at the time and had been diagnosed with autism and other associated conditions.

She served 74 days of her sentence. She had not been in custody before and this was the first time she had been separated from her autistic son. The effects on her son were serious and long-lasting; the entire family found the experience traumatic. On 29th March, she was granted bail. At the High Court the decision of the magistrates to commit her to prison was declared unlawful and was duly quashed. The court found the decision of the magistrates to sentence Mrs Aldous to imprisonment was unlawful on five grounds.

1. The magistrates, in making the enquiry required by regulation 47, must treat each liability order, each year of liability, separately. In this case there was no separate enquiry by the magistrates for each of the separate years of liability. Following an earlier case, that would be fatal to the decision.

2. In respect of each amount there should be an inquiry as to means. In this case, the enquiry was so hopelessly inadequate that it failed to meet the requirements of the regulations; it could not properly be called an enquiry.

3. Regulation 47 stipulates that the court must make an enquiry as to whether the failure to pay is due to wilful refusal or culpable neglect. In making their decision the magistrates should have

taken into account Mrs Aldous' offer to pay £20 per week towards discharging her liability. In failing to give proper weight to that factor the magistrates erred.

4. The purpose of imprisonment under regulation 47 is coercive. There had been no attempt to persuade Mrs Aldous to make the payment in any other way, and there appears to have been no consideration of what period would be appropriate to the purpose of persuading Mrs Aldous to pay. There were other ways in which the local authority might have been able to obtain payment, for example, by attachment to the earnings of her husband.

5. The effect of imprisonment on the children must be considered. In this regard, the court held that although the existence of children cannot absolve a person who should 'properly' be sent to prison, a sentencing court needs to bear in mind what the effect on the children will be; if there are children and if the court does not have the information it needs to assess the effect of the parent's imprisonment on them, then it must make enquiries so that it is properly informed. Those enquiries were not made in this case.

A recent case

In March 2016, a short article (Epstein), that was published in the magazine produced by the charity Women in Prison (http://www.womeninprison.org.uk/). The magazine is sent to all women's prisons. Melanie Woolcock, a single mother, in poor health who was serving a sentence of 81 days for council tax default read the article in October 2016 and wrote to Women in Prison asking for advice. Her case was dealt with by the Centre for Criminal Appeals. Working with the Centre for Criminal Appeals (http://www.criminalappeals.org.uk/). Following a High Court hearing, on 18 January 2017 Lewis J ruled that Ms Woolcock's committal to prison for 81 days was unlawful.

The judgment made it clear that the magistrates had failed to assess Ms Woolcock's financial means and had no basis for concluding her failure to pay was because of 'culpable neglect'. Ms Woolcock of Porthcawl, Wales had been unemployed after working part-time in addition to caring for her school-age child and helping with the care of an elderly neighbour when she fell behind on her council tax payments. She was arrested by bailiffs on 8 August 2016 despite making a payment towards her outstanding debt days earlier. She served 40 days of her prison term.

The Centre is now preparing to intervene in a judicial review of the legality of the current system by which people are committed to prison for non-payment of council tax. Such a challenge would focus on whether the present system violates Article 6 of the European Convention of Human Rights, the right to a fair trial.

Conclusion

Imprisonment for council tax default is generally unlawful because imprisonment is a last resort and other methods should be tried first: the courts can either order attachment from benefits if the debtor is unemployed or from wages/salary if the debtor has a job, and from any savings account if the debtor has neither job nor benefit but has assets, so there is always an alternative. But despite the clear principles established in the legislation, the poll tax cases and *Aldous*, it is vulnerable people such as Amanda Aldous and Melanie Woolcock who are most likely to be sent to prison. As the courts have made clear on many occasions, imprisonment for non-payment of a civil debt should only be used as a last resort. Owing money is not a crime, and imposing any form of punishment is not permitted by law.

See also Epstein, R, (2017) Imprisonment for Debt, In Criminal Law and Justice Weekly Vol. 181, JPN.

http://localgovernmentlawyer.co.uk/index.php?option=com_content&view=article&id=23236%3Aimprisonment-for-council-tax-default&catid=56%3Alitigation-articles&Itemid=24

http://www.criminalappeals.org.uk/blog/2017/1/19/no-longer-in-prison-melanies-sentence-is-quashed

Bibliography.

All Party Parliamentary Group (APPG) (2015) Report on the Inquiry into Preventing Unnecessary Criminalisation of Women' (2015), London.

Baldwin, L. ed/auth (2015) Mothering Justice: Working with Mothers in Criminal and Social Justice Settings, Waterside Press.

Baldwin, L. (2017) Motherhood Disrupted: Reflections of Post-Prison Mothers. Emotion, Space and Society. Elsevier. http://dx.doi.org/10.1016/j.emospa.2017.02.02

Baldwin, L. (2015). Rules of Confinement: Time for Changing the Game. *Criminal Law and Justice Weekly*, 179 (10). https://www.criminallawandjustice.co.uk/features/Rules-Confinement-%E2%80%93Time-Changing-Game

Baldwin, L. (2017 forthcoming), Grandmothering in the Context of Criminal Justice: Grandmothers in Prison and Grandmothers as Carers when a Parent is Imprisoned, journal In Mantas, K. and Dumont, M. (forthcoming) *Grandmothers and Grandmothering: Weaving Creative and Scholarly Perspectives in Honour of our Women Elders (working title). Canada. Demeter Press.*

Baldwin, L. (Forthcoming, 2017) Mothers in prison; 'Tainted love'; The Impact of Prison on Mothering Identity Explored via Mothers' Post Prison Reflections. *Prison Service Journal.*

Bangkok Rules on Women Offenders and Prisoners (2010). Available at: https://www.penalreform.org/wp-content/uploads/2013/07/PRI-Short-Guide-Bangkok-Rules-2013-Web-Final.pdf

Barnardo's (2013). *Working with children with a parent in prison: Messages for practice from two Barnardo's pilot services*, Essex: Barnardo's.

Barnados (2015) *The evaluation of the Community Support for Offenders' Families service,* Essex: Barnados.

Bastick, M. & Townhead, L. (2008). *Women in Prison: A Commentary on the UN Standard Minimum Rules for the Treatment of Prisoners*. Geneva: Quaker United Nations Office

Caddle, D. & Crisp, D. (1997). Imprisoned Women and Mothers. *Home Office Research Study Number 162,* London: Home Office.

Carlen, P. (ed.) (1985). *Criminal Women*. Cambridge: Polity Press.

Carlen, P. (2002). *Women and Punishment: The Struggle for Justice.* Cullompton: Willan.

Chigwada-Bailey, R. (2003). *Black Women's Experiences of Criminal Justice, Race, Gender and Class: A discourse on disadvantage* (Second Edition). Winchester: Waterside Press.

Corston, J. (2007). *The Corston Report: A report by Baroness Jean Corston of a Review of Women with Particular Vulnerabilities in the Criminal Justice System.* London: Home Office.
http://webarchive.nationalarchives.gov.uk/+/homeoffice.gov.uk/documents/corston-report/ : accessed on 21 June 2017.

Corston, J. (2011) Women in the penal System: Second Report on Women with Particular Vulnerabilities in the Criminal Justice System. London. Howard League for Penal Reform. http://howardleague.org/wp-content/uploads/2016/04/Women-in-the-penal-system.pdf : accessed on 21 June 2017.

Convery, U. and Moore, L. (2011) Children of imprisoned parents and their problems, in *Children of Imprisoned Parents*, (Ed) Peter Scharff Smith and Lucy Gampell, European Network for Children of Imprisoned Parents, Denmark.

Epstein, R (2017) Imprisonment for debt, Vol 181, *JPN*, 4 February 2017.

Epstein, R. (2012). Mothers in Prison: The sentencing of mothers and the rights of the child, *Coventry Law Journal.* December 2012 Special Issue: Research Report. http://www.makejusticework.org.uk/wp-content/uploads/Mothers-in-Prison-by-Rona-Epstein.pdf : accessed 21 June 2017.

Galloway, S., Haynes, A., Cuthbert, C. (2014). *An Unfair Sentence—All Babies Count: Spotlight on the Criminal Justice System. London.* Barnardo's and NSPCC http://www.barnardos.org.uk/an-unfair-sentence.pdf: accessed 20 June 2017.

Gelsthorpe, L. & Morris, A. (2002). Women's imprisonment in England and Wales. *Criminal Justice*, 2/3, 277-301.

Gomm, R. (2013). What Will 'Count' And Be Transformed For Women In The Criminal Justice System? *British Journal of Community Justice*, 11(2-3): 153-157

Hedderman, C., Palmer, E. & Hollin, C. (2008). *Implementing Services for Women Offenders and Those 'At Risk' of Offending.* London: Ministry of Justice. http://217.35.77.12/Cb/england/research/pdfs/2008/together-women.pdf

Hedderman, C. & L. Gelsthorpe, (Eds.) (1997). Understanding the Sentencing of Women. *Home Office Research Study 170.* London: Home Office.

Hedderman, C. & Gunby, C. (2013). Diverting women from custody: The importance of understanding Sentencers' perspectives. *Probation Journal,* 60(4) 425–438.

Heidensohn, F. (1981). "Women and the Penal System" in A. Morris and L. Gelsthorpe (Eds.) *Women and Crime,* 129/139 Cropwood Conference No. 13 Cambridge.

House of Commons (2013) Hansard debates: Women's Prisons, https://www.publications.parliament.uk/pa/cm201314/cmhansrd/cm131008/debtext/1310 08-0001.htm

Jordon, S. (2013) Missing voices: Why women engage with, or withdraw from community sentences London Griffins Society. http://www.thegriffinssociety.org/system/files/papers/fullreport/research_report_2013_01. pdf

Masson, I. (2014) *The Long-Term Impact of Short Periods of Imprisonment on Mothers*, PhD Thesis, King's College London. https://kclpure.kcl.ac.uk/portal/en/theses/the-longterm-impact-of-short-periods-of-imprisonment-on-mothers%28eab8d31e-4609-4836-9969-3fe627aff7c5%29.html : accessed 21 June 2017.

McIvor, G. (2004). *Women who offend.* London: Jessica Kingsley Publishers.

Ministry of Justice (2013). *Compendium of reoffending statistics and analysis,* London: Ministry of Justice.

Ministry of Justice/NOMS (2012) *A distinct approach – a guide to working with women offenders* London: Ministry of Justice.

Ministry of Justice (2015). *Population and capacity briefing for Friday.* 15 May *2015,* London: Ministry of Justice.

Minson, S. (2014). *Mitigating Motherhood: A study of the impact of motherhood on sentencing decisions in England and Wales*, Howard League for Penal Reform, London. http://howardleague.org/wp-content/uploads/2016/03/mitigating-motherhood.pdf accessed 20 June 2017

Minson S., Nadine R., Earle, J. Sentencing of Mothers: Improving the sentencing process and outcomes for women with dependent children. Prison Reform Trust.

http://www.prisonreformtrust.org.uk/Portals/0/Documents/sentencing_mothers.pdf   :
accessed 20 June 2017.

Murray, J. & Farrington, D. P. (2008). Effects of Parental Imprisonment on Children, in
M. Tonry, (Ed.) *Crime and Justice: A Review of Research*. Chicago: University of
Chicago.

O'Malley, S., and Devaney, C., (2015) Maintaining the mother–child relationship within
the Irish prison system: the practitioner perspective, Child Care in Practice, 22:1, 20-34,
DOI: 10.1080/13575279.2015.10547 http://dx.doi.org/10.1080/13575279.2015.1054786

O'Malley, S., and Devaney, C., 2016. Supporting Mothers in Ireland with their familial
relationships; a case for the revival of the social work role. Probation Journal 1-17. Sage.
http://www.i-hop.org.uk/app/answers/detail/a_id/796/~/supporting-incarcerated-mothers-
in-ireland-with-their-familial-relationships%3B-a

Player, E. (2005) "The reduction of women's imprisonment in England and Wales: Will
the reform of short prison sentences help?" *Punishment & Society* 7.4 (200,5): 419-439.

Prison Reform Trust (2016) *Prison: The Facts. Bromley Briefings*. Summer 2016. Prison
Reform Trust, London. http://www.prisonreformtrust.org.uk/Publications/Factfile

Prison Reform Trust (2017) Response to the to the Sentencing Council consultation on
breach   guidelines,   Prison   Reform   Trust,   London.
http://www.prisonreformtrust.org.uk/Portals/0/Documents/Consultation%20responses/Se
ntencing%20Council%20consultation%20on%20breach.pdf

Raikes, B. (2016) *Unsung Heroines: Celebrating the care provided by grandmothers for
children with parents in* prison. *Probation Journal*

Robertson, O. (2015) Child rights: some long-term perspectives, in *European Journal of
Parental Imprisonment: An evolving child rights agenda*, Spring 2015.

Trebilcock, J. and *Dockley*, A. (*2015*) 'A very high price to pay?': Transforming
rehabilitation and short prison sentences for women, In: *Women and criminal justice:
From the Corston Report to transforming rehabilitation*. Brayford, J. and Annison, J. and
Deering, J., eds. Policy Press, London.

Wahidin, A (2014) *The Unofficial Story: The Experiences of Former Female Politically
Motivated Republican Prisoners*, Palgrave. Series Editor: Professor John Brewer.
Forthcoming.

Worrall, A. (1990) *Offending Women*, London: Routledge.